CHURCH CAMPING

CHURCH
CAMPING

ADMINISTRATIVE MANUAL FOR
SPONSORING UNITS, PLANNING COMMITTEES,
AND DIRECTORS

BY ROBERT PICKENS DAVIS

ART BY RUTH ENSIGN

JOHN KNOX PRESS
RICHMOND, VIRGINIA

Published especially for use in
  American Baptist Convention
  The Christian Church (Disciples of Christ)
  Church of the Brethren
  Cumberland Presbyterian Church
  The Moravian Church, North
  Presbyterian Church in the United States
  The Presbyterian Church of Canada
  Reformed Church in America
  The United Church of Christ
  The United Methodist Church
  The United Presbyterian Church in the United States of America

Standard Book Number: 8042-1180-9
Library of Congress Catalog Card Number: 70-85427
© M. E. Bratcher 1969
Printed in the United States of America
First Printing

CONTENTS

15 Jan 71

37790

PREFACE

THE SCOPE OF THE MANUAL

Church Camping deals with a particular kind of camping—a church-sponsored experience in group living which makes significant use of natural resources. It therefore does not deal wth campsite management, with work camps (unless they are held at a campsite to work toward its improvement), or with conferences and retreats which happen to be held at a campsite.

It is a manual for administrative leaders. Manuals have been written on camping for various age groups, on such specific types of camping as day camps, on the task of the small-group counselor, etc. This is an attempt to bring together certain common elements of all of these into one manual to serve all phases of church camping by offering help to the sponsoring unit, the planning committee, and the director.

FOR WHOM THE MANUAL IS PREPARED

The sponsoring unit may be a particular congregation (especially in the case of day and family camping, and sometimes of travel camping), but church camping as a rule is sponsored by a larger unit. The unit could be composed of two or more congregations of the same or different denominations; it could be simply a presbytery, diocese, district, etc. of one denomination; or it could be composed of several such official bodies from one or more denominations. However it is constituted, such a unit has some clearcut responsibilities for the camping program. It is not, however, in a position ordinarily to make detailed plans. It therefore delegates many duties to a planning committee.

The planning committee usually is a subcommittee under the major body that deals with the total Christian education program of the sponsoring unit. (In some cases a planning committee could be set up by particular churches or larger groups of churches whose cooperative educational efforts are confined to the camping program. Then the committee must do all it can to relate the camping program to the varied educational programs of those who compose the sponsoring unit.)

The planning committee should be large enough to represent different age groups and interests; it should include more than one high school youth. The size of the committee will vary, depending on the extent of church camping and the assignments given to it. There should be enough members so that no one or two persons will be overloaded. The planning committee may be divided into subcommittees with such assignments as program, leadership recruitment and training, property development, maintenance, and operation. However, in order to keep the committee from getting too large, persons with special gifts may be co-opted to serve for a short time on subcommittees for special assignments. The planning committee will select the actual directors of the camps or one director for all of the camps; in either case the director may have an assistant, selected by the planning committee in consultation with him.

The director can fill any one of three types of roles. (1) He can direct one or more particular sessions of camp, out of numerous sessions which will be held during the year. (2) He can serve for the entire summer season, directing all of the summer camps. (Understandably he would usually be paid for such service.) (3) The third type of director serves the camping program for the whole year. This person is on salary and may have other responsibilities assigned him.

There may be variations of these patterns, but by the title "director" this manual will refer to the person who has direct responsibility for a camp session, whether or not he has in addition all-summer or year-round responsibilities.

THE CONTENTS OF THE MANUAL

Church Camping is the result of a cooperative effort of several denominations (thereby reflecting the fact that the growth of church camping in the past twenty years has been due largely to the splendid relationship existing between denominational leaders as they have worked on the former Committee on Camps and Conferences of the National Council of the Churches of Christ). This is an added reason to pause at this point to underscore the fact that, of necessity, users of *Church Camping* will have to make adaptations to fit their own situations. Camping is by its very nature a flexible program; furthermore, no two denominational structures and no two camping situations are ever identical. Even the terminology may differ. That used herein has been generally agreed upon by the Committee on Camps and Conferences mentioned above.

But there are certain principles and procedures which have proven themselves over the years. Those with administrative responsibilities for camping should be familiar with them, and then deviate from them when they have good reason to do so. This manual begins by proposing a philosophy of church camping, to provide a common stance for all who share in the task. Next, broad policies that must be determined are outlined, with suggestions as to the role of the three administrative groups in fixing policy. In chapter 3 the manual presents the program possibilities open to those who plan camping programs. A chapter on leadership gives job descriptions, along with suggestions for the recruiting and training of leaders. A final chapter outlines month by month the tasks that need to be undertaken if a camping program is to be most effective. An appendix gives sample forms of many types that have proven valuable, and an annotated listing of resources completes the manual.

CHAPTER 1
PHILOSOPHY

Camping is fun! But church camping is much more than fun.

If camp is to mean more in the lives of campers than a happy vacation or release at the moment, it must cause its campers to meet and work out real life situations, and be ready in attitude and skill to face their problems at home, at school, and in the neighborhood.[1]

These are the words of one who had spent most of her camping life working with those whom we would call "disadvantaged" boys and girls. What she says has special significance in a day when church camping, after two decades and more of sensational and almost unquestioned growth, is being seriously reexamined by Christian educators. Those who planned this manual were not unaware of this challenge. But because camping at its best is not just a withdrawal from life but is preparation for living, and because church camping has a unique role as set forth later in this chapter, several denominations have felt it worthwhile to cooperate in producing *Church Camping, an Administrative Manual.*

CHURCH CAMPING IN THE CONTEXT OF THE CHURCH'S MISSION

The purpose of church camping is the same as that of the church: that all persons may respond to God in Jesus Christ, grow in daily fellowship with him, and meet all of life's relationships as children of God.

The forms of camping with which we deal in this piece take people out of the world of men into the world of nature. Nonetheless, they offer a means of fostering Christain growth in order that campers, as was said above, may "meet and work out real life situations, and be ready in attitude and skill to face their problems at home, at school and in the neighborhood."[2]

Camping should never be a retreat from the world; rather, it offers in a unique fashion, as will be spelled out in this chapter, life experiences during camp plus preparation for life in the world. If it is rightly entered into, camping can be mission, to paraphrase Emil Brunner.

CHURCH CAMPING IN THE CONTEXT OF THE CHURCH'S EDUCATIONAL MINISTRY

Church camping professes to be a part of the total program of the church, but only a part of it. The leaders attempt to build the life of the camp community on foundations which have been laid through nurture in the home, the teachings of the church school, and the worship of the congregation. They hope to see the campers return home better equipped to apply Christian truth because they have experienced a vital living relationship to their fellow campers and to the world of nature.

Elements in the camp life which go beyond other teaching opportunities in the church are:

1) length of time. At least in resident and travel camping, campers and leaders share their lives for the full 24 hours of the day for several consecutive days or weeks. Discussions interrupted because of other activities can easily be resumed or may even find their answers in a succeeding activity. There is time for follow-through.

2) *whole of life.* The teaching situation in camp involves everything that happens during the day. Personal habits, interpersonal relationships, meals, play, work, study, and worship are teaching-learning opportunities.

3) *change of pace.* Leaders and campers go apart from the routine of life and center their life in a small group. They give up many things that normally mean much to them and adopt methods of living that are more rustic. They accept a more informal way of life that encourages genuine involvement with a new group of people.

4) *life in community.* Determining activities that are a part of the total program of the camp is the responsibility of the small group. It is true that there are certain limitations to their freedom, but they experience more group decision-making in the camp than they have experienced in most other phases of their lives.

5) *new associations.* Groups which do not normally come together in close or lasting association, such as inter-cultural and inter-racial ones, live together as a unit.

6) *the relational teaching element.* All of the elements above may be centered in this one. The greatest opportunity the leader has is to use his relationship with campers and staff to communicate the Christian faith as it applies in every phase of their life together.

CHURCH CAMPING IN THE CONTEXT OF OTHER CAMPING OPPORTUNITIES

The following factors distinguish church camping from that offered by other groups or agencies:

1) *sponsorship of the church.* This implies that the teachings of the Christian faith are the background and basis for all that takes place in camp. The church recognizes its failures in carrying out these teachings, so it claims for itself only the desire to grow, not the attainment of perfection.

2) *Christian maturity of leadership.* Emphasis is placed on the maturity of all of its leaders, especially the small-group leaders. Since the purpose is living and communicating the Christian faith, the leaders must have a maturity in the faith to be able to share it.

3) the Bible basic. There are many other things to study and to research, but the teachings of the Scriptures are basic in daily living. This means seeking to apply its truth to life at camp and at home, not merely learning facts from or about the Bible.

4) outward expressions of worship. Some forms of corporate and individual worship are a part of the daily planning. This means publicly recognizing God as our life giver and sustainer, and expressing our gratitude to him in a variety of ways and settings.

SPECIAL CONTRIBUTIONS OF CHURCH CAMPING SUMMARIZED

The special contributions of church camping may be summarized as follows:

1) provides a person with a deeper awareness of God as creator and sustainer of the universe
2) relates a person to other persons in a peer group, or families to other families, in Christian living
3) relates younger persons to more mature, adult Christians other than their families, in a sustained, counseling relationship
4) affords an opportunity to study the Scripture and make application in an immediate, living situation
5) affords an opportunity to discover that all of life is holy, and that it cannot be separated into the sacred and the secular
6) encourages the spirit of Christian community cooperation rather than the spirit of competition
7) helps in the development of self-reliance
8) leads to a Christian understanding of the worth of an individual in terms of what he is rather than of what he possesses
9) provides a setting where inter-group activity can take place at a significant level
10) teaches a person to be responsible for the care and use of all of God's creation

CHAPTER 2
ORGANIZATION AND POLICIES

The sponsoring unit, the planning committee, and the director of a particular camp each has the responsibility to determine certain policies (and rules). It is the purpose of this chapter to suggest which policies should be set at which level, so as to avoid conflicts of authority. In so doing *Church Camping* will at times spell out a policy (and occasionally a rule) that has proven itself in some situation; at other times it will simply say that a policy needs to be determined. But even in the former cases the policy-maker should review the suggestions in the light of his own situation, and not simply adopt them automatically.

THE SPONSORING UNIT

DETERMINES ROLE OF CAMPING IN ITS TOTAL MINISTRY

A whole body of persons does not usually rise up and advocate initiating or adopting a program. One person, or a small group of persons, becomes aware of a need and of an opportunity or method to answer the need; he then presents the matter to the group. Now it becomes the responsibility of the whole group to establish the fact of need and the adequacy of suggested methods for meeting the need. The sponsoring unit should delegate such careful study to a small committee, which would bring back full reports. Questions like these would need facing.

What is the apparent need?
Who are to be served?
How can they be served best?
What are others doing to serve them?
Are there other ways of serving which will be adequate?
What will bring the best results?
What should be our program?
What is involved in sponsorship of such a program?

ADOPTS PHILOSOPHY AND BROAD GOALS

If the study committee reports that church camping seems to be a viable answer, it should be asked to recommend a philosophy of church camping and the outlines of broad goals that might feasibly be attained over a given period of time. The financial implications should be included to the fullest extent possible. These recommendations should take into account the needs of persons of all ages and of groups with different interests and backgrounds, all in the light of the total mission of the church. If the report is adopted, the minutes of the sponsoring unit should carry a rather detailed account of the philosophy and the projected goals, to serve as a reference point for the future. However, as the years pass these should be altered in the light of experience and changing needs.

GIVES FINANCIAL SUPPORT

The sponsoring unit should understand the cost of camping and determine policies for underwriting it. A budget might be divided into several categories: immediate needs, ongoing needs, and long-range needs. The immediate needs might include employing a director, renting facilities or acquiring land and developing a site, securing equipment and supplies, and providing for leadership training, promotion, insurance, and operation. Ongoing needs will include such things as salaries of paid staff, leadership training, promotion, operation and maintenance of the facilities and site, and care and replacement of equipment and supplies. Long-range needs might include capital investments to expand the facilities and site for an expanding program, replacement of facilities, and salaries for additional staff.

The sponsoring unit also needs to set the policy for financing individual camp sessions and make this clear to the planning committee. It should indicate what part of the expenses must be covered by the fees charged campers and other groups using the facilities. It should set a policy on insurance, in order to be certain that proper liability, health, and accident insurance is provided.

DELEGATES AUTHORITY

It is quite obvious that the sponsoring unit must delegate authority to a smaller group, which will be called in this manual the planning committee. It must have responsibility for both the site and the program, in order to have the whole operation unified.

Those who have made the original study and recommendations might become the nucleus of the planning committee, but this is not always wise. The sponsoring unit should see to it that this committee has on it someone who is knowledgeable about the characteristics of each potential group of campers and about what other programs are available for them. Two or more young people should be included. Since decisions about administration and finance, buildings and grounds, and public relations will be made regularly, people with ability in these areas will be needed. A balance between laity and clergy is of utmost importance.

RECEIVES REPORTS

A full annual report should be presented to the sponsoring unit. The unit itself will indicate what is to be included in this report. A financial statement, statistics regarding those served, and some evaluation of the program and staff are a minimum. An evaluation of the facilities in light of future needs should be in the annual report from time to time. Less elaborate reports may be requested between annual reports, and the planning committee may wish to take the initiative in communicating with the sponsoring unit.

THE PLANNING COMMITTEE

WORKS OUT OBJECTIVES

The planning committee, the composition of which is suggested on page 17, will take the philosophy of church camping and the general goals adopted and work out long-range and intermediate objectives which will lead to these goals. Thus, it may be envisioned that church camping should reach a certain percentage of a particular age group of the sponsoring unit and that a given percent of campers should be persons who are not in any church. The program may be limited to small numbers of a particular age group at the beginning, but the goals that are set should encourage steady expansion.

Goals and objectives should be evaluated constantly against a changing society, changing needs, and changing church programs. They should be altered when this seems advisable. The camping philosophy also should be reviewed regularly and revised as necessary. Objectives should be stated in terms of what it is hoped campers will do rather than of what leaders will do. Manageable objectives are preferable to broad, intangible ones.

The scope of the total camping program should be determined by the needs of the constituents of the sponsoring unit and of the communities included in it. Suggestions from denominational boards and agencies about different types of experiences should be given serious consideration. Available resources may be a determining factor in what is planned.

DETERMINES QUALIFICATIONS FOR STAFF

The planning committee should determine the qualifications of members of the staff. Where there is a full-time director, the committee will do well to work closely with him in defining the qualifications of other staff, since he, as its agent, will deal directly with staff. A job description for the director should be written by the planning committee, and then he should work with the committee in preparing other job descriptions. (See details in chapter 4.)

A subcommittee should be given responsibility for recruiting staff and planning for their training. It must work closely with the directors of the camp sessions. (See chapter 4.)

SETS POLICIES

A policy is a course of action chosen to guide and determine decisions in order to reach given objectives. A rule is a prescribed guide for conduct or action in a given situation. Policies for the camp should be made so that there will be flexibility. Rules tend to be rigid, so there should be as few rules as possible. The planning committee needs to set the policies under which directors and their staffs work. Some of the major areas for policies are:

1) progression. The planning committee needs to see its responsibility for all age groups and to plan progression in program. *Grades 4–6:* Day camping may be adequate for these younger children, though resident camping for a week, with most of the activities taking place around the small-group living area, may serve the older elementary grade campers, and some are experimenting with fourth-grade residence camping. *Grades 7–8:* Resident camping with activities more challenging to the physical and mental ability of the camper and including an overnight experience at an outpost site should appeal to junior highs. The time span of the camping experience might be extended to ten days to two weeks. *Grade 9:* The middle high camper usually does best just with his own grade, though some prefer to combine ninth- and tenth-graders. Activities that challenge the imaginations and abilities of this group must be provided, including discussions of more serious topics. Some of the travel camp ideas, such as backpacking, canoeing, and spending time at other sites, should be planned on a limited scale. *Grades 10–12:* The senior highs have a tendency to lose interest in camping unless something quite different is planned. They are able and willing to give themselves in service in work camps. They are quite able to plan and carry out plans under adequate leadership in experiences of trailer traveling, backpacking, canoeing, cycling, etc. *Young adults* can participate in the same type of experiences as senior highs, but they are frequently limited to weekend camping. *Families* (see pp. 55 ff.) need special consideration because of the age ranges. Camping for many will be for extended weekends, but others will want a full week or more. *Middle and older adults* should be given a place in camping. Facilities that are suitable for youth may not be acceptable for older adults, but many of the middle adults can use them.

2) grouping and leader ratio. The preceding paragraph has given some clue to groupings. The public school pattern of your area may help determine your principles of grouping, if there is any uniformity in pattern. Your denomination may have recommendations based on the way leader and camper materials are prepared.

In a day camp, grades four and five or grades five and six combine well. If all three grades are included, it may be wise to place them in small groups within the camp as nearly as possible according to school grades.

In a resident camp, grades five and six, the last two years of elementary school, make a good combination. If fourth graders are included, they can be combined with the fifth grade group, while the sixth grade forms a separate camp, or all campers can be put in small groups according to grades. However, some camps are experimenting with broader age ranges, such as fourth- through ninth-graders in the same camp and the same small groups. Planning committees need to be flexible and aware of changing patterns.

As is the principle in education, the younger the pupil the higher the ratio of leaders. This is essential in camping, where the child's whole life is related to his counselor for the length of the camp. For the junior-age camper, there should be a small-group leader for each four campers, and the maximum is five campers to one leader. The ratio of campers to leaders may be a little higher in day camping, but the small group must not be so large as to hinder good relationships and good educational principles.

Grades seven and eight combine for good working relationships. If several camps are scheduled for these grades, it may be wise to plan some camps for individual grades, with one or two for combined grades. If the ninth-grade group is to be combined with grades seven and eight, try to put them in separate small groups within the camp, so they can plan within their ability range without being held back by the younger campers.

There should be one adult leader for five campers in a shelter group. If there are more girls than boys, do not have over five in a girls' shelter group, and have less than five in each boys' group. In some camps where the numbers of one sex are much larger than of the other, a small-group camp has been formed of all one sex. This is not the best policy. When it is followed, a leader of the other sex should be attached to the group during the day. It is better to divide the minority sex evenly among the small groups, with a minimum of two campers of a sex to a group. You may consider a registration policy that will limit the number of both sexes in each session of camp, with the understanding that some camps may be cancelled if registrations of either sex is too small. This will require early registrations so campers may be changed to another session of their choice.

Limiting the small group to ten boys and girls plus their two leaders keeps the group to a better working size for educational opportunities and interpersonal relationships. Each person will have a chance to participate in activities, and the leaders can observe special abilities to be encouraged and needs to be met.

The camper-counselor ratio for a middle high (ninth-grade) camp is five to one. When the ratio is larger, the individuals and the group tend to suffer. The small-group leaders may have a tendency to distort or even bypass democratic principles in decision-making because of the length of time required for so many to participate.

Grades ten, eleven, and twelve are the senior high school group, though in a summer program the high school graduate may be included with young adults because his work limits his time for camping. The type of camp planned will determine the size of the small group; i.e., some travel camps must have small numbers in each group. Six campers plus the leaders might be considered a minimal group size, with twelve persons, *including* leaders, the maximum.

The leadership ratio for senior highs will also vary according to the type of camp. It is most desirable to have men and women leaders. A work camp will often require, in addition to small-group leaders, skilled persons to direct the work. Travel camps should have an extra leader besides the two small-group leaders, who may double as a resource person.

Before moving on to post-high-school campers, stress should again be laid on the importance of flexibility. For instance, when inner-city youngsters come to camp, to be isolated from others from their "turf" can be devastating.

This manual will consider those persons who have graduated from high school to be young adults. Older adulthood may begin at about sixty years of age. The type of program planned for each group will determine the size of the group. Discussion and work groups will function better when the number ranges between eight and twelve persons.

Adult groups do not need small-group leaders in the same sense younger campers do. They do need resource persons to help them in planning and to help in special ways at camp. Leadership may be found in their own age group. Thus, the availability of skills for the work that is needed may be the basis for organizing a work camp; or a hiking, canoeing, or boating enthusiast may spark the desire for a travel camp. The planning committee, however, must check to be sure that the necessary leadership skills are there.

3) scheduling. The schedule for use of the camp facilities must be made early. The subcommittee responsible for schedules might have two stated meetings a year. At a meeting not later than mid-October, the committee should review all activities on the camp calendar and determine the schedule for the following summer. The committee might set its second stated meeting in late winter, to schedule activities for the following fall and winter. Authority can be given to the full-time camp director or some other person to schedule activities where there is still an opening, or to change the schedule when necessary.

Camps and other experiences can be scheduled to give a variety of choices. Instead of running three camps for juniors consecutively, for example, allow time for one or two youth camps or a family camp between them. Scheduling should take into consideration prevailing vacation patterns of families so that no potential campers will regularly be left out because their camp always comes at the same time in the summer. Summer patterns of youth activities, such as summer school and job opportunities, should influence the scheduling of youth camps. School schedules already have set patterns for the summertime, and it is possible that the whole camping picture may be affected soon by new patterns of school schedules. Keep in close touch with the school authorities in order to know ahead of time changes in school scheduling. Be aware of all the school systems in the bounds of the sponsoring unit to avoid scheduling some groups out of the program.

4) literature. The choice of materials to be used as teaching aids is the planning committee's responsibility. A list of those published cooperatively and by the denominations is in the Resource section (pp. 137 ff.). If possible, the directors should have a voice in determining what is to be used, but the decision should be made by the planning committee in accord with policies set by the sponsoring unit.

A library of resource aids should be carefully chosen by the planning committee or one(s) it designates to do this. A policy should be set for times when the director wishes to get material, and consultation is not feasible. The important thing is to furnish the camp a basic library that will help the director and small-group leaders do their jobs.

5) public relations. Public relations can be divided into four categories: with the community, with businesses, with the churches, and with the campers and parents.

The committee should know the community in which the camp operates. The resident director should be encouraged to participate in community organizations. If the camp is going to deviate from local practices —as by employing persons of differing races, integrating races in camp, or housing boys and girls in shelters close to one another—work out a plan to inform the neighbors about the facts of and reasons for camp policies. Let them learn the truth from you rather than hear false rumors.

See that the boundaries of the property are clearly marked. Know which neighbors are congenial and which are not, and work to resolve misunderstandings and conflict. Be sure that all directors understand relationships with the neighbors. If a neighbor's property is to be used in any way, get written permission from him. Invite neighbors in for a special meal at least once during the year to share what is happening; they might also attend a worship service.

See that everything possible is done to avoid being a nuisance. The road into camp can be a tension spot. It may have been considered a private road before the camp was established; often the camp traffic causes more dust or ruts than local people had before. Garbage and trash disposal should meet the health standards published by The American Camping Association. By fire regulations and drills seek to guarantee that the camp is not a threat to the neighbors. Noise should be kept under control, particularly if there is not a buffer zone between camp and the neighbors.

Consider the camp's responsibility as a beneficiary of taxes. The normal attitude is to have camp property declared tax-exempt as a part of the church. Legally this may be correct, but it may not be wise to have the entire acreage declared tax-exempt, especially if some of the land is used for farming or pasturage. Good public relations are difficult for a non-taxpayer. The camp might make an annual contribution to some of the tax-supported services, such as the fire department, county agent, or conservation office, in appreciation for services rendered.

Good business practices are part of our Christian witness. The life of the camp depends on relationships with business firms—food deliverers, utility services, equipment repairmen, and deliverers of building supplies. See that the manager keeps good records and that the bills are paid promptly. See that the access road to camp is adequate.

Another lifeline of camp is the churches. The planning committee must minister to their needs and keep them informed. The agents may be the leaders and the campers, but the committee has an active responsibility, too. See that reports to the sponsoring unit are clear and interesting. Take advantage of opportunities to make presentations in the churches and to organizations of the churches and of the sponsoring unit.

The camp clientele are campers and their parents. What the committee does in assisting these persons to have a happy camping experience is one form of good public relations. Here staff are the real agents of the committee. Policies need to be provided the director and staff to govern relationships with parents in reference to visiting during the camp session, contacts in case of illness or other trouble, receiving calls from and calling home, and follow-up contacts after the camp.

6) promotion. A subcommittee of the planning committee should handle promotion, unless there is a paid staff who can take responsibility. Some of the ways for promoting are the annual brochure, posters for bulletin boards, letters to former campers, campers' letters to themselves, pictures of camping (movies, slides, and snapshots), reports to the sponsoring unit, special days at the campsite, and talks before groups in local churches. Some of these have already been mentioned or are very obvious. Let us look more closely at a few of them.

Mail the brochure soon enough for camps to be included in family plans. A frontpiece on the brochure might become a trademark for the camp. The artwork should be good, but it should not be used so long that it loses its impact. Where photographs are used, show active camping scenes rather than campers looking at the camera; a picture is to tell a story. Do not use photographs of persons for more than two seasons; try to keep them current each year. Be sure that no photograph will be embarrassing to a person.

Include important data in the brochure, but leave details to another communication. Emphasize that this is part of the program of the local church. Make it clear who are to attend the various sessions, and give registration procedures so the registrar will not have to refuse those too young or too old. Be specific as to dates and hours of the beginning and the closing; stress that campers are to be present for the entire period. Give clear directions as to the location of the camp. State briefly the policy about visitors during camp, unless a letter is to be sent by the registrar to each parent. The mailing address is important. The telephone number for emergency calls should be listed, along with a policy statement about telephone calls.

Posters for church bulletin boards should be clear as to dates and who are eligible to attend, but too much print will make them hard to read, and they will be bypassed. Color is an eyecatcher. Posters should be sent to each church at least two months before the registration deadline, but preferably earlier.

Some camp directors have each camper write himself a letter at the close of the session, and these are mailed during the winter when he should begin thinking of camp again. One director takes a picture of each small group and mails a copy to each member of the group along with schedule and registration blanks for the coming summer. An extra schedule and registration blank should be included for a friend who did not attend the past year.

The story that a movie or set of color slides tells of camp, along with a taped recording of music and camp sounds, is an excellent promotional method. The pictures must be good and the recording applicable to the story being told. Ordinarily this audio-visual should be used only one year. This can become an expensive undertaking and it should not be attempted unless it is to be done well. It can be used effectively in a gathering of prospective campers and their parents, with former campers and their parents serving as hosts.

Each time you get a group to visit the campsite, you have a promotional opportunity, but do not let it interfere with the program of camp. Indeed, visits might better be encouraged at other times than during the resident camp sessions. When arrangements have been made for a meal, visitors should follow the family style service of the regular camps.

7) registrations. The policy for registering campers should be uniform. It is wise to have one person at one address receive all registrations. See sample blank in the appendix, page 106. Some camps prefer to have an application blank sent in first, after which the registrar mails a registration form to be filled out. This is followed by a letter of acceptance in the director's name, and the health blank (see appendix, p. 115), with directions on filling it out and instructions to bring it to camp. This letter can carry more details about the camp—what to bring in the way of clothes, bedding, and toiletries; equipment and musical instruments; reading and study aids. It should also mention some things *not to bring*. The policy about food from home should be stated clearly.

The registrar should keep each director informed as to the number of campers and should send names and addresses to him as soon as possible. He needs to be thinking about grouping campers and leaders.

8) health and safety. Policies relative to health and safety must be based on state health department requirements. The American Camping Association standards should be used to supplement these. (See appendix, pp. 113 ff.)

It is impossible to remove all hazards from a campsite, and to do so would not be desirable, for that would destroy some of the most attractive areas. On the other hand, precautions can be taken. Poisonous plants might be eliminated in places of great camper activity by spraying with weed killer or by grubbing. Other areas can be posted to warn campers to stay out. Natural habitats for poisonous snakes and insects can be cleaned out in some areas of camp. Care must be taken not to upset the balance of nature, thereby permitting other pests to increase to the nuisance stage. Rustic rails or fences might be set at precipices or steep banks on the edge of deep water. Roads might be rerouted away from natural travel patterns of campers. Mine shafts and cave entrances might be covered or fenced.

The health and welfare of campers and staff is of utmost importance. Some camps may find it difficult to get a registered nurse, but the lack of one can be a serious matter. Every staff person should be encouraged to become a Red Cross accredited first-aider or advanced first-aider, though this cannot replace having a registered nurse.

9) site and resources. The planning committee will determine where the camp is to be held. If the sponsoring unit owns an adequate site, this question is solved for resident camps. Day camps, travel camps, and family camps may be held at other places than church-owned sites. Where another site than its own is to be used, the committee must learn what facilities are required and search out land that can best meet these needs, keeping in mind health and safety standards. Where travel camps are planned, permission must be gotten for all uses of private property.

The planning committee responsible for developing and maintaining a site for the total camping program should study *Site Selection and Development: Camps, Conferences, Retreats* by Bone, et al. Where using its own property, the committee should check with the management to see that all facilities are ready before the camping season opens. Then periodic checks can be made during the year to be sure all is being kept in order. Instruct each director to check over the facilities, equipment, and supplies before the opening of camp, to be sure he will have what is needed, and to check at the end of camp to help those who follow. When two or more camps are running at the same time, careful planning will insure that all groups have what is needed when they need it.

The planning committee should set policies on the use of the property, making the rules clear for keeping the buildings in order and the land and woods in good condition. This is doubly true if, in order to make full use of the site, it proves wise to rent to other groups beyond those of the sponsoring unit.

10) reports and evaluations. The planning committee should show the directors, when they are asked to serve, what kind of reports and evaluations it requires by giving them a copy of the forms to be used: evaluations of site, program, staff, and potential directors. If these are too simple they are valueless, if too detailed they are frustrating. Study the completed reports from year to year to be sure the questions are clear. Set a deadline when the reports are due, preferably a week or two following camp.

Two or three persons should study and collate the reports and evaluations before the meeting of the committee. If answers are not clear, the director(s) should be queried. Directors might be invited to discuss the reports with the planning committee or with the ones who are collating reports. From these reports, needs are listed and plans for the coming year are made. They serve as the basis for part of the report to the sponsoring unit.

The evaluations should say something about the effectiveness of individual leaders without being hurtful to one who may not have done as well as expected; under different circumstances or with a different co-leader the person might perform most acceptably, or the experience of this year might make him an excellent leader next year. A confidential record of these evaluations should be kept by the recruitment chairman or in the office of the executive of the sponsoring unit.

11) thanks. Most directors do not need a note of thanks, because they are happy over a job well done, but it is such extra thoughtfulness that makes directors willing to serve again. It is more important to write a note of thanks to the governing body of the director's church to let it and the congregation know what has been done and how much it is appreciated. This applies to lay leadership as well as the ordained, because such service represents a congregation serving the larger church.

SUPERVISES FINANCIAL PROGRAM

The planning committee should be responsible for the total budget of the camp, which has been provided by the sponsoring committee, including capital investment and operations. If the sponsoring unit has not set a policy specifying that the camp must be or need not be self-sustaining by the fees which are charged, the planning committee should recommend a policy on this matter. The planning committee also should ask for a policy for raising capital and for receiving and spending special gifts. It should see that an adequate bookkeeping system is set up (see appendix, p. 122), and that all funds are handled by responsible persons. It should, with the sponsoring unit, work out a budget that is realistic and adequate for expanding operations and replacing worn out or obsolete equipment and materials. The budget should be divided into two parts: capital investment and operations.

Capital Investments

1) land. Land acquisition should take into consideration the possibility of using the site fifty years or more without depleting the natural resources. Each committee should keep extending its horizons to meet expanding opportunities and changes in the surroundings. This may mean adding to the original purchase or seeking additional sites.

2) utilities, roads, fences. These items are part of the original site development, but as new areas are opened, additions will be needed.

3) buildings. Let program dictate what buildings will be erected. Build for flexibility of use, but do not sacrifice particular needs to flexibility. For example, the health lodge should not be made inadequate for its primary purpose just so it can also serve as a retreat center during cold weather, nor should the dining lodge be less than satisfactory just so it can double as a sleeping shelter/dining room part of the year.

4) equipment. Remember that some basic farm and road-type equipment is necessary to keep the property in condition. The waterfront construction and equipment—docks, shelter, boats, and canoes—are capital investment. The library should be provided. Basic equipment for travel camping—trailers, tents, tarps, pack racks, cooking and eating utensils—should be added as demands arise. An annual item should be included in the budget for equipment, and it should be allowed to accumulate if it is not used.

Operations

1) salaries. All salaries paid in connection with the camp should be included in the budget unless they are paid from other budgets of the sponsoring unit (such as the salary for a director of Christian education who directs the camping program). The following persons might be included: director, office and bookkeeping staff, manager, grounds superintendent and his helpers, food services staff, the nurse, waterfront staff, resource persons, and small-group leaders.

Along with salaries such benefit services should be included as social security, hospitalization, life insurance, retirement, and housing allowance.

2) maintenance. Include such things as building repairs and painting, utility repairs, road maintenance, erosion prevention and correction, reseeding and reforestation, swimming pool and lake maintenance, repairs to beds and mattresses, laundering linens and mattress covers, repairs to broken equipment, etc.

3) replacing equipment. Captial investment provides equipment, but its replacement is operating cost. Normal wear and breakage must be anticipated. This includes everything from heavy farm and kitchen equipment to canvas shelters and small tools in the craft shop.

4) program. This includes expenses for items ranging from publicity and promotion to postage for follow-up on campers after camp. Training of leaders might be included, or this might be a separate item. Books and charts for staff and campers (exclusive of the library), purchase or rental of audio-visual aids, and art and craft materials are some of the items to be included.

5) supplies. Supplies are those things which are used up without recovery possibilities, such as paper, paste, paints, soap, insecticides, disinfectants, oil, kerosene, turpentine, and medical necessities. If craft supplies are furnished, determine how they will be purchased by campers. Since stock must be purchased ahead of camp, a budget item is needed, even though the cost may later be recovered.

6) food. A camp that is well fed has already made a good start toward being a happy, successful camp. A capable dietitian will help greatly in making the budget for food. This will be one of the large items in the budget, but camper fees will balance it out.

7) transportation. Travel funds will be needed by the director to set up and to operate the camp. The manager will have travel expenses. Volunteer workers in various parts of the program will have travel and room and board expenses. Training events will demand travel, though this might be charged to training expenses. Where there is travel for campers to the doctor, to special events, or to mountains and streams for hiking and boating, or if there is motor travel camping, these items might be included under transportation or under program.

8) insurance. Have a professional insurance agent give counsel on insurance, and if one who has dealt with camps is available, seek his advice above others. See that adequate insurance coverage is carried at all times. This might be divided into four categories:

liability, including general liability insurance on the site, automobile liability, and workmen's compensation

property damage, covering loss of building and shelters or their contents, loss through theft and dishonesty, loss of camper's personal property, and physical damage to automobiles

income protection, covering such things as loss of fees because for some reason the camp cannot open, and extra expenses incurred by emergencies, such as having to close camp before the end of the season or having to keep campers extra days because of a quarantine.

medical (accident and sickness), covering each camper and staff member not covered by workmen's compensation, even for those in weekend or one-day sessions. The nominal cost for this is usually added to the fee of each camper. This gives protection while traveling to and from camp as well as while in camp; it also covers treatments that are required within several months after camp for camp-incurred problems.

It may be necessary in some states to protect the planning committee and sponsoring unit with a liability policy. It would be wise everywhere to investigate the advantage of package plan comprehensive coverage.

9) reserve fund. Every budget should carry a reserve fund to take care of large expenditures necessitated by breakdown or wearing out of equipment, or loss of facilities which are not adequately covered by insurance. A percentage of the annual income, possibly five percent, should be set aside. It should be invested and allowed to accumulate until needed.

If the committee is paying larger interest on a loan than the interest rate available on the invested reserve fund, there will be a tendency to use the reserve fund to pay the debt. Be prepared in some way, then, to meet large emergency expenditures on the camp.

THE DIRECTOR

RELATIONSHIP TO THE SPONSORING UNIT

The director is under the supervision of the planning committee, and only through it is he related to the sponsoring unit. Suggestions or adverse criticisms from members of the sponsoring unit should be made to him only through the planning committee. If he has suggestions and criticisms relevant to the work of the sponsoring unit, he approaches it through the planning committee. Only in rare circumstances will he appeal from this committee to the sponsoring unit.

RELATIONSHIP TO THE PLANNING COMMITTEE

The director should study what has been said above about the planning committee's responsibilities, so that he can see his role in the light of it. If the committee has not made his relationship to it clear, he turns to the chairman with his questions. He needs to know who is responsible and can answer his requests if the chairman is not available.

The director must know and endorse the philosophy of camping as approved by the sponsoring unit. If he has questions about the planning committee's goals, objectives, or policies, the committee should answer them. If the committee has been shortsighted in setting them, the director should help it adopt better ones. His ideas should be compatible with the policies of the planning committee. The director is an interpreter of policy to his staff and the campers; he is not a maker of policy. He helps his staff transform policy into program.

RELATIONSHIP TO THE PERMANENT STAFF

The director should understand the job descriptions for all the staff. These should define not only tasks but also the relationships among the staff, i.e., who supervises whom. Questions for clarification are directed to the planning committee rather than to staff members. Further understanding of relationships will come while working with the staff.

The director arranges with the resident manager for a visit to the camp and has him show him around and introduce him to the resident staff. He should discuss procedures that relate him to the manager and his staff, in order to be part of their team and to get them to be a part of his.

He should go through the buildings with the manager. If changes are desired, he finds out if the manager can arrange for them or if a request should go to the planning committee. He is alert to find things to compliment. He learns about the housekeeping responsibilities of the campers. If adjustments seem advisable, such as giving more jobs to campers, setting up special work tasks, or reducing some jobs, he works out plans before meeting with his staff. He gets specific directions for the use and care of canvas. He visits the bath houses and latrines and discusses the procedures for cleaning them.

While walking over as much of the site as possible, he asks the manager to point our special areas of interest and danger spots. They discuss the policy for gathering fire wood and for building fires. (It may be that charcoal is the best fuel for camp cookouts.) Basic conservation practices with relation to cutting in the woods, gathering craft materials, making new paths, and destroying hornet nests, reptiles, and animals, are discussed. If viewpoints differ, discussion may be an education for both.

He checks the equipment the campers are to use. If there are broken or dull tools, he asks to have them put in good condition. It may be that staff and campers can profit by doing some of this during camp. He finds out how equipment is to be requisitioned by the small groups. If some equipment is missing, he finds out if the manager can get what is needed, or if a request to the planning committee is necessary.

He checks everything possible about food services. He visits the kitchen and pantry and makes notes about health practices. He discusses menus with the dietitian, if possible, and gets an understanding of her budget and her requirements. He goes over procedures for meal service and cleaning the dinning room. He gets copies of the forms to be used for cookout orders and snacks. He gets all the information possible about cookout practices, such as ordering procedures for groups, picking up food orders, sanitizing dishes in small-group camps, disposing of garbage, and returning unused foods to the trading post or the kitchen.

He works out the schedule for precamp training sessions at the campsite. He makes it clear that the manager is a member of the team, that he is wanted at staff training, and that he is a resource person for the camp. Other members of the permanent staff should be included in precamp training and should be invited through the manager—the dietitian, the health counselor, the waterfront director, and possibly others.

RELATIONSHIP TO THE VOLUNTEER OR SUMMER STAFF

The success of the camp will depend largely on the relationship of the director to his staff before the opening of camp. This will be treated in chapter 4 under Recruitment and Training. A director who selects and trains his staff well will have a much easier time during the camp session.

RELATIONSHIP TO PROGRAM

The word "program" is filled with many images. One definition is "a plan or procedure: a schedule or system under which action may be taken toward a desired goal." The church camp program is the sum total of all activities, planned and unplanned, which are related to or participated in at camp; some would even include the impact of the experience. Program begins with the initial planning, and it continues in selection of staff and resource materials, in promotion, in leadership training, and in the camp experience and follow-up.

1) literature. The director's relationship to selecting leaders' guides has already been mentioned (p. 31). It is assumed that a library is available. He should be alert to new books, pamphlets, and magazine articles and recommend those most needed for purchase. It is good to discuss new materials with other directors in order to have the best available and to keep all directors up-to-date.

2) promotion. The director should have little to do with promotion (unless he is full-time director) other than furnishing data on leadership. But he may find that he has full responsibility for it. He should be sure promotional material is mailed at least two months before the deadline for closing registrations, or three to four months before the opening of the camp. The same is true of fall, winter, or spring events. He makes use of several means of promotion—the printed and the spoken word and audio-visuals.

If the director is responsible for registering his own campers, he should set up a system so that all applications can be acknowledged promptly. If someone else is the registrar, he should get information on the campers as soon as possible in order to learn the names and to make personal contact with them before they get to camp.

3) finances. The director should not be seriously involved in handling funds if the sponsoring unit owns the facilities and has a central registration plan. If he is responsible for registering campers and is using rented facilities, he may have much more to handle. The planning committee should outline clearly the duties of the director with regard to finances. The director then makes up a budget with the funds allotted, or makes up a budget and presents it to the committee for its approval. He sets up a bookkeeping system that can be audited at the end of camp. He pays bills by check whenever possible, and where this is not done he gets receipts for all expenditures. He tries to have all equipment and supplies purchased through the camp account and paid for by the regular camp treasurer.

He should check with the small-group leaders and resource leaders several weeks before camp to see what supplies will be needed. He clears with the planning committee which of these will be available, how much can be spent on purchasing supplies, who will make the purchases, what the budget limit is, and how bookkeeping will show the expenditures.

4) interpreting policies. The small-group leaders need freedom in planning and carrying out plans for the camp, but they need a framework within which to plan. The planning committee can set this framework of policies and thus relieve the staff from criticisms. Some policies and rules that have proved valuable are suggested, but variation will be inevitable in light of particular sites, staffs, length of camp, etc.

a) the store. Where meals are well planned and prepared, and opportunity is given to supplement these with snacks planned by small groups, there is no need to operate a store selling candies, soft drinks, and the like. Diet can be controlled better and meals are eaten better where there is no store. Its absence eliminates the necessity for campers to have pocket change (which becomes a temptation for some to steal) or for a bookkeeping system where deposits are made and a card punch system is used to keep a record of purchases. Special arrangements may be made to have a small supply of tooth brushes, tooth paste, soap, tissues, postcards, and flashlight batteries in the administrative office.

b) food from home. In short-term camps, the campers do not expect boxes of food from home, but sometimes they arrive with a supply of candy and gum. Make it clear that such foods are not to be brought. If they are, or if a box arrives during camp, the director should determine whether to hold it until the end of camp or to have it opened and shared with the small group at a meal or snack time. Parents should be informed of the policy, particularly when a birthday comes during camp. The cook or the small group can bake a birthday cake, but too much attention to a birthday may make those who do not have one during camp feel neglected.

c) radios, etc. Transistor radios are not needed in camp. They are a disturbance for those who wish to sleep during rest hour, and they sometimes create conflict because of anticipation of particular programs. The staff does not need them either. A daily newspaper should be available, and daily reports on world news should be made to the entire camp. Weather signs can be learned and a daily report made from an improvised weather station.

It may be necessary to say that portable TV sets and record players are to be left at home or, if brought to camp, retained in the office.

d) dining room service. The quality and quantity of food, along with dining room behavior, are keys to a happy camp experience. It is good for members of the planning committee occasionally to drop in at meal times as unexpected guests to learn what the meals are like. The director and staff should give a frank evaluation of the meals, remembering that the budget the planning committee provided is a determining factor in food services.

Mealtime should be a time for communion and fellowship as well as for satisfying the need for food. Therefore, it behooves the director to give attention to a plan for meal serving which will foster both ends. The plans for table service should be uniform for all camps, so that staff and campers will know what to expect.

It is not possible in this manual to outline a plan for food services that will fit every camp dining room, but some policies can be stated which should help determine rules. Let the main principle be that thoughtful and gracious consideration for others is basic to good manners and to Christian living.

When each camper and leader shares in the responsibility for table serving, he gains an appreciation for a service which he will enjoy all through his life. He comes to recognize its worth but also its problems, and he should develop patience when he does not get everything he wants at the moment he wants it. In the camp, to have all share in the work helps break down barriers which are prone to rise when some are assigned table service as scholarship aid.

Size and shape of tables is important. A round or square table that will seat six to eight persons is best for camp. Each shelter group can be assigned a table and still have space for a visitor or two when desired. The number of persons per table is kept at a workable size for serving plates family style. The relationship of person to person is good, so all can participate without loud talking. Rectangular tables seating more than six persons encourage more than one conversation during the meal or require loud talk if all are to hear.

A dining room hostess is a great help in food services. After checking with the dietitian to know what the menu is, she can post a copy of the menu and have a place setting out as a display for table setters to follow, indicating the dishes and serving pieces needed. She can offer assistance to the table setters and waiters when she sees that they need it.

The method of food serving and waiting on the table will help to create (or destroy) a desirable atmosphere. If a table host serves the plates, younger campers are not forced to pass large platters of hot food, it is easier to divide the food proportionately, and campers are encouraged to eat some of everything served. If one person gives attention to serving and one brings food from the kitchen, and all wait to start eating until each has been served, all are encouraged to join in conversation. Where the campers are large enough to serve as hosts, it is good training for them to take turns at this and not always leave it to the small-group leader.

One person should be designated at each table to serve as waiter. He may be the table setter who comes fifteen minutes early to set the table. He should bring all foods from the kitchen and is the only one to go for refills of dishes. He brings the beverage and places it for a designated person to pour. He returns the dishes of food to the kitchen at the end of the meal and then clears the table of soiled plates by scraping and stacking them at a serving table provided for this purpose. This method may take longer than having each stack his own dishes and rush to the kitchen, or having the dishes scraped and passed around the table, but this is a program of teaching good table manners which are sometimes lacking in our "cafeteria society" and of encouraging the art of table conversation and a relaxed atmosphere.

Singing, telling jokes to the entire dining room, and antics during mealtime are hindrances to good eating habits and digestion. Be firm about such rules. Singing may follow the meal, but it should be planned and led by a designated person. This does not eliminate requests for special numbers, but it can keep the quality of singing on a higher tone.

Some of the leaders' guides give dining room service details. If what you have chosen does not, then get the sheet, "A Recommended Plan of Table Service," from the camp packet published by the General Board of Education of the United Methodist Church.

The policies of dining room service should be used in small-group cook-outs as nearly as possible. It is the job of the director to emphasize this and to set the pattern in the staff training cookouts.

e) total camp meals attendance. Some camps require that all groups eat a certain meal each day in the dining room. One reason given is that this will assure each person of at least one balanced meal daily. But if the menus are checked by the dietitian and the small-group leaders are competent campers, the meals in the small-group camps will be balanced. Planning for cookouts with balanced meals, well prepared and attractively served, is good training for the campers and is fun as well.

Another reason given is to be sure that announcements reach everyone. However, there are other ways to get announcements to groups than to make them at meals. In fact, the fewer announcements made at meal time, the better for all.

While each director may be given freedom to determine the rules for his camp, it is wiser for the planning committee to set definite policies, though leaving them as flexible as possible. The kitchen staff needs to understand the policies and rules in order to make food service operations as smooth as possible.

f) cleanup responsibilities. If the camp is to serve to the fullest as an educational and training experience, campers should participate in keeping the camp clean and in order. It is necessary to sweep daily the dining room and lodge, and to keep the bath houses and latrines clean. Discourage dropping litter, and encourage everyone to pick it up when he sees it. The wood supply needs replenishing for the fireplace in the lodge and at the campfire circle. These are jobs campers can do, and it is training that may serve well back home. When staff and campers recognize this concern as camp policy, the director has an easier time building it into program, which at camp includes meeting the needs of daily living and giving service to others.

g) cutting in the woods. Some campsites may be without trees; others have so few that they must be guarded. On these sites, charcoal or other materials are necessary for fuel. Care must be taken even in heavily wooded sites to be good stewards of the natural resources. All leaders need to know the principles of conservation and care of the forests. Emphasize the ground rules for gathering and cutting firewood. Use wood that is dead and already down as much as possible. Fell only dead trees. Gather poles and sticks of green wood only in designated areas away from the small-group camps. Seek advice from the director and camp superintendent when there is doubt about what to cut. Leaders and campers can learn much about ecology (the pattern of relationships between organisms and their environment) in seeking firewood as they learn of the possibility of destroying homes and feeding places of insects, animals, and birds.

The staff should be informed each year of changes in policy. In order to keep trees and forests for future camps, slabs may be hauled in for firewood, acreage planted for saplings, and reforestation made a regular part of campsite stewardship.

h) Sunday activities. Policies need to be clear at this point. Different denominations or sections of the country will have quite varied ideas on the subject. So will individuals: When campers report home, some parents may think camp has been too liberal, while others may think it was too strict. Some camps avoid the dilemma by starting with supper on Sunday or at midmorning Monday and closing by early afternoon Saturday. However, Sunday can be a richly rewarding day in camp when the small group has its own Bible study for its Sunday church school, and for worship either the total camp gathers for a simple service appropriate to the setting, or each small group plans its own service. Sunday that comes toward the end of camp usually can have more meaning than one early in the camp, because it can be camper planned.

Limits may be set for activities such as swimming, boating, and games, but help the staff understand the reasons, so they can interpret the policies to the campers. Toward the end of camp, Sunday, with its quieter activities, can provide a welcome rest.

1) the director's role during camp. If the director has selected and trained his staff well, he may have a quiet time during camp. His work may revolve around the following three areas.

a) administration. The small-group leaders and the campers are the key to program planning during camp; the director makes his greatest contribution during the pre-camp training periods. Needs for supplies and equipment which were not anticipated may arise, and the director should be ready to help obtain them or give a satisfactory reason why they are not available. The director must stand as the liaison person between the permanent staff and his staff.

At times there may be conflict between small groups over use of equipment and facilities. The director may be able to mediate in such situations to the satisfaction of all parties. There will be times when several groups, or the total camp, will wish to be together for something special in worship or recreation. The director can serve as leader of a planning group for this, while the small-group leaders continue to work with the rest of their groups. It is not necessary and may not be desirable for the director to preside or be the speaker at total camp activities.

The director is the contact person with parents in cases of accident or sickness. If it should be necessary for him to take a camper home, he should designate a specific person to act as director during his absence. He also might be the one to receive all calls from parents during camp and to supervise all outgoing calls of campers.

b) counseling. The director is the counselor to his staff. The pre-camp training period is the time for personality adjustment of leader to leader, but the best efforts to pair leaders does not always work. Adults, however, hesitate to admit poor relationships with co-workers. Sometimes the director can sense feelings of tension. When he does, he should make an opportunity to discuss with the parties concerned what he feels. He should be available most of the time for his staff to come to him to discuss problems before they get out of hand.

The director is a counselor to the campers only if a small-group leader refers a camper to him. He must work through his staff to give them confidence and to help the campers have confidence in them. The director should not let the permanent staff bring grievances to him that should go to the manager or directly to the planning committee.

c) resource person. It is hoped that every camp director will have some field of specialty that will make him welcome in a small group. It may be in planning and construction in the small-group area, nature study or crafts, compassing or star study, cooking, story telling or singing, Bible study, or planning for outdoor worship. He need not know all of these. The small-group leaders could suggest that he be invited to visit and work with their group. The director should not be offended if he is not invited into each group but should rejoice in the abilities of his staff.

CHAPTER 3
PROGRAM
POSSIBILITIES

Church Camping obviously cannot provide administrative leaders with all the detailed information they need on the five types of camping described in this chapter. It does seek to acquaint sponsoring units and planning committees with the scope of the small-group, out-of-doors camping program that they can potentially offer; in addition, some specific suggestions are given, but these are no substitute for the details that can be found in the more specialized materials listed in the Resources.

The simplest way to treat the various church camping programs is to avoid elaborate classification systems and simply to consider them under five general headings: day, resident, travel, work, and family camps.

There can of course be such combinations as a family day camp or a resident work camp.

DAY CAMPING

WHAT IS DAY CAMPING?

The title gives the definition. It is camping during the day only, with the campers returning home for the night. The American Camping Association definition is: "Organized Day Camping is an experience in group living in a natural environment. It is sustained experience carried on in the daytime under the supervision of trained leadership."[2]

Mrs. Maude Dryden, who has been called the godmother of the day camp movement, made this comment: "Day camping is such a flexible plan that a variation of it can be suited to almost any condition, always being based on its principle function, that of leading back to simple, leavening pleasures of the woods and streams, and blue skies."[3]

WHO SPONSORS DAY CAMPING?

Day camping can be sponsored by one church if the membership is large enough to provide six to twelve persons of the age group which is to camp, plus the leadership required. Often two or more churches of the same or different denominations will plan together. (This is a good place for ecumenical cooperation.) The maximum size of the total day camp should be the same as that of a resident camp, about forty campers (assuming area and equipment will permit this). A day camp, however, can be much smaller than a resident camp and not work a financial burden, because it involves less overhead expenses.

Day camping has a valid place because of its contribution to the growth of the camper; it is not merely preparation for resident camping. Indeed, it is the only camping experience some will have. For this reason, every camp planning committee should consider the program seriously, find out what is happening in its area, and lend a helping hand to the churches which might be conducting camps. There are three distinct ways help might be offered.

A *workshop* on day camping might be sponsored to introduce leaders to its potential, to interpret materials that could be used, and to train persons in some of the skills. Much of the workshop can be held in a church in town during the day hours which would be spent in camping, provided one or two days are spent at the campsite. Another approach would be to sponsor a *laboratory day camp* to train leaders. An experienced leader would be with each small group, and two or three trainees would work with him. The leaders and trainees would meet two days before the opening of camp and plan together. Each day following the camp, they would meet to evaluate what happened that day and to review plans for the following day. At times, some of the trainees would assume the leader role while others would be observers. Finally, there may be times when the planning committee will *actually plan and conduct day camping* because of the particular needs of a group or the lack of leadership among the churches. This should not be allowed to become an easy way out for those churches that have leadership and can conduct their own camps.

WHERE IS IT HELD?

Transportation is a determining factor in the location of day camps. A rule of thumb to be applied is that the site should require no more than forty-five minutes to one hour travel from the departure place. A New York City camp director commented: "This just about puts us in Central Park." Large metropolitan areas obviously must make adjustments. However, some city parks *are* open to day camping and might well serve the purpose if there can be a camping program, not just the use of the park's swings, slides, and ball fields.

Some churches have purchased enough land so that a day camp can be held at the church. Others have purchased property a few miles out in the country for expanded church activities. Church members in the country might lend their meadows and woods for day camping. Some church-owned campsites are near enough to a number of city and rural churches for them to camp on this property. Some sponsoring units recognize that they need to provide for as many churches as possible, so they purchase smaller sites suitable for day camping within travel range of churches which cannot go to the main campsite.

FOR WHOM IS DAY CAMPING SPONSORED?

Day camping originally was planned for elementary children who were not ready to be away from home overnight. This emphasis has continued to a large extent in independent, institutional, and church camps. It need not be so confined, for it can meet other needs. Day camping can be planned for junior highs who cannot be included in the resident camp program because of lack of space or because of lack of money to pay the cost of resident camping.

A day camp work camp can be planned for senior highs and adults, with the day extending for longer hours in order for them to include study and fellowship other than that gained in working together. (We must recognize that a nonresident work camp can become more of a service project than a camp.)

Family camping might well be adapted to a day camp experience where facilities are not available for resident family camping. The camp day could begin a little later in the morning and extend later in the afternoon, with the evening meal being cooked at the campsite. As the families develop their living areas, they might keep in mind that one night could be a sleep-out, if the weather is not threatening or if temporary canvas shelter can be provided. If all members of the family do not feel that they would like to sleep out under the stars, it still would be a family project to plan for and support those who do wish to do so.

Day camping with older adults may meet a growing need when facilities are not suitable or not available for resident camping (for example, the usual camp mattresses and beds may not be comfortable for older adults). Chairs or cots can be provided for daytime rest. The older adults would function in small groups, as in other church camping, but they would need resource persons rather than small-group leaders.

WHAT ARE THE UNIQUE OPPORTUNITIES OF DAY CAMPING?

Facilities

Fewer and less expensive facilities are needed for a day camp program than for resident camping. Basically, there should be toilet and hand-washing facilities, shelter for refuge from sudden rains, a fireplace to add warmth on cool days, a place and facilities for the rest period, a cooking area, and a place for storing equipment and supplies. The toilet facilities might be pit latrines and the hand-washing facilities can be made from No. 10 tin cans or gallon plastic jugs. The shelter against rain might be a simple roof held up by solid block pillars or wooden posts; a large tarpaulin hung over a ridge pole between two trees or a large tent, if there are no trees, could also serve. Any of these could also serve as shelter from the sun during the rest period, or mats on the ground under the shade of trees would suffice.

The cooking area need be no more than a spot cleared of combustible materials or, where firewood is not available, a charcoal stove. Many ingenious substitutes for elaborate fireplaces might be considered. The storage place can be the trunk of a car, the back of a station wagon, a large wooden box (rodent- and water-proof), or a building erected for this purpose.

The water supply is of prime importance. Open springs are to be avoided because of the danger of pollution. If such a water supply is used, some purifying element should be used regularly. Clear water from a stream, with a purifying element added, may be used for hand washing, and drinking water can be transported to the site. Necessary refrigeration can be supplied by ice chests.

Small equipment such as saws, axes, steel files, rakes, shovels, and a few craft tools represent a small investment in comparison with heavier tools and equipment which are needed on a resident campsite. These should be purchased for the day camp and not borrowed from individuals. The equipment list and supplies will depend on the plans of the leaders, their imagination, and the resources of the site.

Since housing and board are not required for the leadership, the registration charges need not be as large as in resident camping, though transportation charges may be larger.

Leadership

Since the day camp is often sponsored by a single church, the planning committee from the church usually is acquainted with the leadership from which to choose. They know those who work best with the age group and also know some who cannot serve every Sunday but who can give a block of time during the year. It is quite valuable to have leaders from among those who work regularly with the campers because they already know and understand them. There is also a carry-over value in that they will continue to work with the same youngsters in the church school through the year. Even in a laboratory day camp, the planning committee will depend on some leadership from the church from which the campers come.

The leader with family responsibilities is at home to see that breakfast is served and is back home in time to prepare the evening meal. The weekend is not involved. In these respects, it is easier to serve in a day camp than a resident camp.

Planning and training for a day camp are done mainly in in-town meetings at the church or in homes. This makes it easier for leaders to get together. Shorter periods of time can be given to planning because the staff can get together more often. Co-leaders can confer over the telephone when questions arise. Where printed resource materials are scarce, they can be shared more easily. Cooperative training with other churches and agencies (YMCA, etc.) is very often possible.

Program Possibilities

Program possibilities are as broad as the imagination of the leaders and campers and the natural resources of the setting, though what is planned must of course fit into a shorter time span than that provided by resident camping. Suggestions from leaders' guides for resident church camping can be adapted. There are other program suggestions in books on day camping. See Resources, p. 134.

Contributions

1) Day camping is another opportunity to foster Christian growth.
2) It witnesses to the camper that the church cares enough to plan something special for him.
3) It takes boys and girls out from the classroom, where they often feel completely hemmed in and therefore resist learning, and gives them freedom of space, of action, and of expression.
4) Working with the same leaders and members of the peer group for several hours each day for five to ten days provides time to develop relationships through which a camper may come to know himself better.
5) Longer periods of study in an environment which is more appealing to the young campers allow for depth of search, frequent return to the subject with a slightly different approach, and the application of the study to daily living.
6) There develops a fellowship within the church on which other experiences can be built.
7) It offers a chance for some to camp who cannot attend a resident camp. This makes it possible to reach more persons with church camping.
8) It offers a sense of security to boys and girls who are not ready to be away from home overnight.
9) It offers an evangelistic approach to boys and girls who have not been interested in the work of the church but who are attracted by the natural appeal of outdoor activities and of fellowship with their peer group. They will attend a camp, whereas they will not attend church school. Here they can come to feel the Christian concern of church people and the love of God for them as persons and for their families.
10) The fact that camp clothes are everyday clothes removes the status symbols of dress.
11) It provides a chance to camp when overnight facilities are not available.
12) It provides a chance for older adults to enjoy sustained fellowship with a group, while returning to their own sleeping quarters for the night.

13) It gives families an opportunity to enjoy limited camping experience as a family and in relationship with other families, without the expense of owning camp equipment.

RESIDENT CAMPING

Organized resident camping is defined by the American Camping Association as

an experience in group living in a natural environment. It is a sustained experience under the supervision of trained leaders. Camping provides a creative educational experience in cooperative group living in the out-of-doors. It utilizes the resources of the natural surroundings to contribute significantly to mental, physical, social and spiritual growth.[4]

For church camping we might paraphrase this definition as follows:

Church resident camping is an experience in group living in an outdoor setting sponsored and directed by the church as a phase of its total educational program and under the supervision of mature Christian leadership. It utilizes the resources of the natural surroundings, interpersonal relationships, and the teachings of the Scriptures to contribute significantly to mental, physical, social, and spiritual growth.

Resident church camping has developed along the lines set down by the late L. B. Sharp, founder and director of the Outdoor Education Association, who saw great educational values in camping. He described his method, decentralized camping, as

. . . the organization of campers into small "family" groups of eight or nine, with two co-leaders. Each such unit is responsible, as far as possible, for its own program, welfare, and way of camping. Each unit becomes a small camp that has a life, a unity, and a character of its own, but receives guidance and leadership from the directorship of the whole camp.[5]

Decentralized camping in the church has become known as small-group camping. Ideally, it involves small groups composed of the same number of boys and girls with a man and a woman leader, or of several families with a leader-family. The group is a working unit which has a large degree of independence in planning and carrying out its own activities within a given framework and in relation to other small groups. In other words, while it has its self-identity, it also must identify itself with other small groups as a part of the whole camp. Three to six small groups of peers or families make up a camp. More than one camp may be functioning on the site at the same time, but their programs should not overlap, unless to the extent of all eating in the dining lodge at the same time, if this is necessary.

Resident camping is the type of program most people think of immediately when camping is mentioned; it is listed simply so that it will be seen in the context of the variety of program possibilities available. Almost all of the material in the other chapters of this manual speak relevantly to resident camping, so no additional data are needed here.

TRAVEL CAMPING

WHAT IS TRAVEL CAMPING?

Travel camping is simply camping along the route of travel. The purpose is the same as in other church-sponsored camping: that each person may respond to God in Jesus Christ, grow in daily fellowship with him, and increasingly meet all of life's relationships as a child of God. The concern is to bring about the individual's Christian growth within a Christian community, rather than just to cover space or to see beautiful or historic sites.

Church travel camping can be hiking, horseback riding, hiking with pack animals, bicycling, canoeing, and driving in cars with trailers. Hiking, canoeing, and using trailers are probably most popular.

WHO SPONSORS TRAVEL CAMPING?

What has already been said about sponsoring units and planning committees applies here. In travel camping it is especially important for the planning committee to know what the purpose is, why this is to be a part of its camping program, and whether it has competent leadership. To have competent leadership requires having an adequate number of leaders who know what they are doing, where they are going, and the group with which they will be working.

WHERE ARE TRAVEL CAMPS HELD?

One must recognize that the world is the field today, or at least the parts of the world open for easy travel: the United States, Canada, Mexico, and Europe. But each camp begins from a designated spot, a building or campsite of the sponsoring unit.

Famous hiking trails are the Appalachian Trail, running along the crest of the mountains that stretch from Maine to Georgia, trails in the high Sierras, and trails in the mountains of the Northwest. If these are too far away to be considered, get county maps or geological survey maps and plan a trail along little traveled roads in scenic parts of the country, or plan a cross-country compass course. Bicycle hiking might use some of this same route, with more hard-surfaced roads included and greater distances covered.

There is no limit to where trailers can go, from campsites near the large cities to remote sites in state and national parks. Church-owned sites across the country might be opened to trailer travelers by writing ahead and making appointments for specific nights. (Some do not welcome overnight camp visitors.)

Wilderness areas of the West are ideally suited for burro and horseback travel because there are outfitters who can supply the animals, special gear, and guides.

Minnesota and Canada are famous for canoe travel, but canoe trips can be taken throughout the United States, except in the high mountains. (It is wise to avoid large lakes, where winds frequently cause waves and white caps, and lakes where speed boats abound, unless the canoeists will stay close to shore most of the time.) Streams with some rapids, and quiet streams of the plains and tidewater sections are ideal canoe ways.

FOR WHOM ARE TRAVEL CAMPS PLANNED?

Travel camping fits into the plan of progression in church camping and should be planned for ninth- to tenth-graders through adults. Juniors and junior highs can enjoy one- or two-day trips from the base camp, often not going off the grounds of the campsite, but they should not be included in planned travel camps of several days' duration. Short travel camps might be planned for the ninth- and tenth-graders, with several days spent at the base camp studying the route, planning menus, assembling and packing equipment, and getting to know each other as a cooperating, working group. The real strength of travel camping is with the eleventh- and twelfth-graders and younger adults. They have more ability to plan and carry out their plans, more endurance for hardships frequently met, and more sense of community in accepting each other as persons.

WHAT ARE THE UNIQUE OPPORTUNITIES
AND CONTRIBUTIONS OF TRAVEL CAMPING?

It is a challenge to campers and leaders to meet new situations. There may be loads to carry, mountains to climb, streams to master, and weather conditions to meet; but most of all it means living with a group of people in a setting and situation where the worth of each is of vital importance to the life of the group. This is no place for the shirker or the self-centered egotist. Here each should come to feel that he can open his heart and reveal himself without fear of group condemnation. Here each may develop in a supporting community a new sense of his worth.

Travel camping offers an opportunity for a person to develop a wholesome sense of dependence upon the group and an independence from many things and ideas which have ruled his life. Faced with the wilderness and the few possessions which are to protect him and sustain life, a person can begin a reevaluation of what is important to him. Persons can take on a greater measure of importance.

The study and worship time of travel camp can push the group back to a depth consideration of what is around them and within them. Some pre-camp preparation should be made on the study theme, for reference books are left behind except in trailer travel. It is necessary for each to think through the issue and to formulate his ideas so he can express them clearly for himself and the group. Worship experiences grow out of feelings of the group.

It is hoped that the travel camp will be a coed group with about the same number of boys and girls. Working together in the tasks of camping, sharing in the loads that are to be carried, and coming to understand each other in the life of the community can add a new depth of mutual appreciation. The presence of boys and girls brings out the finer nature of each other.

SPECIAL EQUIPMENT NEEDED IN TRAVEL CAMPING

Hiking and Canoeing

Careful planning is essential here, as everything has to be carried either on one's back or in a canoe (and if there is portaging on the canoe trip, all supplies will have to be carried on one's back part of the time). Campers must be prepared for emergencies as well as equipped with food, clothing, and other supplies to last the duration of the trip. Lists of essential equipment and supplies should be compiled after studying the resource materials listed on pp. 134, 135; they should be carefully reviewed and, if possible, checked by an experienced camper.

Trailer Travel

Because supplies are carried for the campers, there is somewhat more freedom than in hiking or canoeing, but even here space and weight are matters of concern. Therefore what is said in the paragraph immediately above applies here also. For help in planning see resources listed on p. 134.

Trailer travel does create particular problems about what to wear. The route that has been chosen and the stops anticipated will determine the clothing. It should be informal but still genteel. One set of dress clothes (jacket and slacks for men and a dress for the women) should be standard clothing for visiting museums, art galleries, schools, and churches. Camp clothing is in order the rest of the time. Always be aware that clothing worn around a campfire becomes heavy with a smoke odor that may be offensive to others. Carry sufficient clothes to keep respectable.

Because of the possibility of sudden showers or several days of rain, rain gear should be waterproof and of a quality that will both hold up while camping and be suitable for appearing in public. All should have overshoes or rain boots.

Even though riding much of the time, there will be sight-seeing and also walking at the campsites. A comfortable pair of walking shoes and heavy socks are needed. If short trail hikes are anticipated, bring suitable footwear.

CAMPSITE WORK CAMPS

WHAT IS A CAMPSITE WORK CAMP?

A work camp is a group of persons living together for a definite period of time in order to accomplish, or take steps toward accomplishing, a particular project within their ability. Because this manual deals only with camping which "makes significant use of natural resources" (p. 7), it treats only work camps which are held at a campsite for the purpose of working to improve it. Those interested in such valuable efforts as inner-city work camps, etc., will need to refer to the Resource listing for help (p. 134). Because of the narrow focus, the work camp described here involves physical labor rather than rendering such services as directing a day camp, a vacation church school, or a community recreation program.

The key to all work camps is the community life of the group. This is partly expressed in the project-related activity, but it also includes the total experience of the group in taking care of its living arrangements, in (often) planning and preparing its own meals, and in planning and participating in study, worship, and recreation.

The project is planned by or with others and is accepted by the group as its task. The project must be one that meets a real need, so that the work will give dignity to the workers as they are assured that they are not just a free labor pool but are rather ministers of God on behalf of those who will use the site in months and years to come.

WHO SPONSORS AND PLANS SUCH A WORK CAMP?

The only group which can sponsor this type of work camp is the sponsoring unit which controls the campsite. The details of its responsibilities as spelled out on pages 16–17 apply to work camps as well as to other types of church camping.

Under the sponsoring unit, the planning committee carries out its particular tasks (pp. 18–30). Each work camp should have its objective and goals which are set in relation to that particular camp. The planning committee needs to be aware of some considerations that are especially relevant to a work camp:

—all professional camp staff (full-time director, camp manager, etc.) working closely with the planning committee
—special care in publicity, so all applicants and parents will understand fully what is involved and what is expected of participants
—recommendations secured from others than parents and pastors for each applicant, to help determine maturity, ability, and emotional stability
—equipment and supplies provided as needed for the particular project
—living arrangements available that are acceptable to the group and that meet health and safety standards
—a budget set up that adequately provides for this distinctive type of camp

WHO PARTICIPATES IN WORK CAMPS?

Participation in a work camp requires a certain degree of physical, mental, and emotional maturity. For this reason, participation is best limited to eleventh- and twelfth-graders and adults. It is possible that some work camps, because of the nature of relationships and physical skill required, should be only open to those of college age and older. There are some projects which are suitable for older adults, including retired people, who have the required energy and skills.

Work camps might cross peer groups and bring together persons of all ages. When this is the case, special attention may be needed in planning for study and recreation.

The work camp size will be determined by the project to be adopted. It is good to have a coed camp working in small group units, with a leader for every seven campers and with both men and women leaders. Adults may not need coed leadership. The tasks should be such that each participant, including the leaders, will be able to spend four to six hours a day in work. The community living responsibilities should be divided among members of the group so each will take his turn at the various jobs. Plans should be made so all are working at the same time and are thus free to rest, play, study, and worship together.

LEADERSHIP FOR A WORK CAMP

The Director

The sections dealing with the work of the director found on pages 30–39 give many responsibilities which apply to the work camp director. On the other hand, he may have such qualifications and duties as these, which are peculiar to his work camp situation:

—has a fair to good knowledge of and skill in the work that is to be done in the camp
—has close working relationship with the planning committee
—helps interpret the program to the sponsoring unit and to potential work campers
—helps the planning committee screen applications whenever possible
—serves as one of the resource leaders in study and worship
—directs the evaluation process daily and at the close of camp, helping the participants make application of this experience to their home situation

The Small-Group Leaders

His responsibilities will be to:

—counsel with his campers
—work with his campers as one of them
—help them plan their work, set goals for the day, and evaluate their progress
—plan with them in their community life duties
—give guidance in planning study, worship, and recreation, and provide leadership as it becomes necessary
—keep in close contact with the director at all times
—be a resource specialist also, if possible

The Resource Specialist

Each resource specialist should have skills suitable to the demands of the project, some knowledge of the age group with which he is working, and the ability to work with them. He should be a full-time member of the work camp, participating fully in the life of the camp community. If the project is a large one with several small groups, each working on a different phase of the project, more than one resource specialist may be needed. He must direct the group in the work and not do the major part of the work himself while just using the group as helpers.

Other Staff Needed

What is said on pages 67–79) about the manager, physician, nurse, lifeguard, cook (if the work camp doesn't do its own cooking), etc., applies, with appropriate adjustment, to the campsite work camp.

CONTRIBUTIONS OF THE WORK CAMP

A work camp serves three distinct groups: the ones who will use the campsite, the ones doing the work, and the churches of the work campers. These are some of the contributions to each group.

Those who will use the campsite benefit by
—being warmed by an awareness of the extent of the concern for them that some people have
—being made more conscious of the sacrifice involved in providing them with a camp experience
—using the improved facilities resulting from the work camp

Those working benefit by
—forming relationships with a new group or deeper relationships with a familiar group
—gaining new knowledge of their potential role in meeting human need
—developing new skills to meet needs
—gaining satisfaction in serving
—finding their personal faith strengthened
—realizing in a new way the worth of persons
—understanding more clearly the dignity of work

The church of the participants benefits by
—receiving participants who have grown toward maturity

—having dramatized before them a lesson on the mission of service

—feeling a sense of involvement in mission through those who represented the congregation in this service

—gaining a better knowledge of the needs and importance of the camp program

The question of who benefits most from a work camp has often been discussed. In many cases, those who participate have felt that they benefited more than the ones they served. But beware lest a work camp degenerate into a "do-gooder" program for the self-satisfaction of the campers and staff. Let the work and its results be of genuine value.

FAMILY CAMPING

Ten years ago a professional campsite master planner designed a church camp and did not include family camping, except as regular camping facilities might be used by families. He is now amazed at his lack of foresight and is redesigning the master plan. A camp program consultant used to ask committees if they could afford a special family camp area; today he asks them if they can afford not to provide such an area. Increasingly the church is awakening to the value and demands of family camping.

We might recognize three distinct types of family camping: a family going on a trip with no relationship to the church program, a group of families from the church planning as a unit for their camping trip, and a church-sponsored and organized program for a group of families going camping. Our concern here is with the last of these.

THE PURPOSE OF CHURCH FAMILY CAMPING

Family camping has a significant role to play within the church's total ministry to families. Experience has shown that such aspects of this ministry as family communication, husband-wife and parent-child relationships, family worship, and ungraded Bible study can be dealt with more effectively in a camping (or conference) setting than in classes or seminars in the local church. Hence the church would do well to program part of its family ministry in the setting of family camping.

Family camping has been defined as an adventure in outdoor living in which the family exercises its ingenuity in providing shelter, preparing food, and enjoying the natural environment. Add the purpose of the church, that persons may come to know themselves anew as children of God in Jesus Christ and grow more mature in this knowledge day by day, and you have church family camping. (This paragraph should be supplemented by what was said in chapter 2 about the philosophy of church camping.)

One main purpose of family camping is to draw the family together as a unit; therefore the entire family should be included if at all possible. In some instances families are also motivated by the desire to have a family vacation as inexpensively as possible, but the underlying concern is still for a deeper family unity. They may be seeking an opportunity to play together, but to accomplish this they find they must plan, study, and work together. It is hoped that in the process the family will take a new look at itself, and that it will be able to return to the normal tensions of its society with a new determination to function as a cooperating unit.

The setting of camp, unless the family is traveling in a modern trailer with every home convenience, will call forth ingenuity in providing shelter, preparing food, and planning for study and recreation. People will become independent of many things which have seemed absolute necessities. They will become dependent on one another and on the members of their camp community. They should become more appreciative of the natural world and leisure in contrast to the city and rush. The natural environment should help them gain a fuller awareness of God as creator and sustainer of the universe.

THE PLANNING COMMITTEE OF THE SPONSORING UNIT

One of the distinct features of the family camp is that it serves best a local church or a group of closely related churches. It should be administered by a family camp committee from this church or group of churches. What then is the responsibility of the planning committee of the sponsoring unit that administers the church-owned campsite?

Since family camping is an important part of the total program of church camping, the planning committee should see that time is allowed in the schedule for those churches which would like to use the site. If facilities are not adequate for family camping, they should be provided as soon as possible, but only after careful study.

The planning committee should promote family camping among the churches. One of the best ways to do this is to plan a laboratory camp, including two families from each of several churches, who can return and plan together for their church. It may be necessary to conduct several such camps to train leader-families in all the churches which are interested. Another way to train leader-families is to get churches which hold family camps to include one or two outside families in their camps and then to assist them in planning for their own church.

THE FAMILY CAMP COMMITTEE OF THE LOCAL CHURCH(ES)

The family camp committee should take a look at the three types of family camping. For individual families who go camping it could suggest a variety of study, reading, devotional, and programing materials to enrich their experience. For a group of families who are planning to camp together, it could offer the help of a member of the committee as a resource person while they plan. It also should be responsible for clearing schedule with the church-owned campsite, if it is to be used.

For the church-sponsored family camp, the family camp committee will function as the planning committee of a resident camp. It will write out the purpose and suggest policies relating to administration and program. These should be presented to the governing body of the church for approval, and they then become the guidelines for the family camp.

It is important that the family camp committee work closely with whatever groups are responsible for family nurture in the participating churches, and that it draw upon resources offered by the denominational office to supplement what is said in this manual.

ADMINISTRATION

Length of the Camp

The length of a family camp will be determined by several factors. A major one is the amount of time parents can be away from their responsibilities.

The distance families must travel may be another factor in scheduling; it is not wise for families to have to travel a full day to reach the site and another day to return home and stay only a day and a half in camp. Finally, finances will influence its length; the cost needs to be kept to a reasonable figure so all families who wish to participate can do so.

It would be well to plan the camp for a full week since it takes several days for people to get to know one another well enough to relax and express themselves freely. An extended weekend, one more day than Friday evening to Sunday evening, should be the minimum length.

Where to Go

Possibilities for camp locations include the church-owned campsite, private camps, state and national parks, or private property, where bath and toilet facilites meet health standards. The principle question in selecting a site is whether or not it meets health standards. (This does not mean that it has all modern conveniences.) See that water, food handling and serving, and sewage disposal are adequate. If they are not, postpone the family camp until proper arrangements can be made.

Families with seventh-graders and up may wish to stretch the camping experience beyond a single site. Three or four families might plan to go on a trailer travel camp, to backpack on a trail, to take a canoe trip or a horseback trip into the wilderness country, or to bicycle on infrequently traveled roads close to home. Be sure that overnight stops are made with permission of the owners of the land.

Number of Families

As few as three or four families can hold a very effective group family camp. The maximum number of families should be about twelve. This will mean a group of about fifty to sixty persons, which is not too large for each to get to know the others.

The group should organize itself to help accomplish the purpose of the camp. A council could be set up with a representative on it from each family; it would suggest total group activities and would relay to all what families are doing individually and what the group will do to-gether.

Another plan is to organize the camp in colony groups of three to four families, with one family as the leader-family. Each colony would select one or two representatives to a council, to function as described above. The colony group would work as a unit, but this does not mean that all the families will do the same thing at the same time. The colony might plan a cookout for all of them, or one or two families might plan their own cookouts while others go to the dining room. The role of the leader-family would be to assist in pre-camp planning, to host the group on arrival and lead in plans for the first twenty-four hours, to give leadership during camp when it has not emerged from the group, and to participate in evaluating and making recommendations for future camps. Colony organization in family camping should not prevent families from fellow-ship with other families in the total camp, but it can foster depth of relationship among those in the same colony.

Grouping of Families

Family camping should be open to every family in the church. It offers an excellent opportunity to assimilate new families into the fellow-ship of the congregation. However, since the number of families in a camp is limited, some way of determining who will go should be devised. Families with children within a similar age range are usually more con-genial and have mutual interests. This helps in study and discussions, while children find companionship with those of their own age. Single-parent families have much in common and sometimes find being together more congenial than being with two-parent families. Middle adult and grandparent families might be grouped together.

But sometimes a cross section of families is the best idea. Children without grandparents and grandparent-age adults without grandchildren can be a complement to each other. Single-person families need to be included in the family camp, but not as baby sitters! Sometimes they can serve best as special resource persons because of their skills, but they should be included with the families and not set apart.

Housing

The housing of families must be as family units, with each having its own privacy for sleeping, dressing, family discussions, and devotions. This may be in cabins on an established site. It may be in canvas shelters such as teepees, hogans, covered wagon, or tents. In some cases, the family may require two shelters as close together as rooms in a house. Some families may bring their own camp shelters and set them up at designated places. Where there is a family camping area on the site, a church may reserve the entire area (or a section of it that can function as a separate camp unit) and have all bring their camping equipment. The group will share in the bathhouse facilities, the dining lodge, the all-purpose building, the craft shop, and the swimming area. A worship area may be set apart for family camp use.

Dormitory living which separates the family into male and female groups is not suitable for a family camp. Look for another place, or plan another type program.

Leadership

The material here should be supplemented with appropriate material from chapter 4. The family camp committee should have on it some who know family camping and possibly some who will attend the camp being planned. They select a family to serve as director-family, and that whole family is involved insofar as the children are able. If there is a leadership training session on family camping, the committee arranges for financing the director-family's attendance. If books are needed, the committee will arrange for their purchase.

The director-family then assumes responsibility, along with the family camp committee, for choosing and training other leader-families. Where the colony plan is followed, a leader-family is chosen for each colony. Other resource persons or families will be chosen according to the program of the camp. The nurse and lifeguard of the campsite should serve the family camp. When a site is used which does not have a lifeguard, a person other than a member of one of the families should be engaged for that duty.

The director sets up a schedule for pre-camp planning and training for the leadership team. The first meeting, held during the winter, might include only the adults for a discussion of philosophy, organization, leadership needs, and books that might be of help. The couples would carry this information to their families and begin their preparation. A meeting for all members of the leader-families would follow a few weeks later. Several in-town meetings might be held in the winter and spring.

The entire staff should go to the campsite about a month before the opening of camp to spend a day or a day and night. This would give them a chance to become familiar with the camp in general and to look for places of special interest. A cookout would be in order. At this time they might review the registrations to become familiar with all the families who plan to attend and particularly with those in their own colony.

Twenty-four hours before the opening of camp the leader-families should arrive and settle in their shelters. Some matters which have been discussed might be reviewed, such as

—registration and housing plans
—health standards and procedures
—waterfront activities and safety practices
—meal schedule and dining room procedures
—food requisitions for cookouts and snacks
—wood gathering, tree cutting, and fire building
—camp cleanup and chores
—use of tools, recreation equipment, the library, and supplies
—a framework of plans to help the group begin making plans
—closing-day procedures and evaluation

The plans for the first twenty-four hours should be such that the campers will have a sense of security in knowing that plans have been made. But these plans must not be so ironclad that they cannot be changed when it becomes evident that change is needed.

Finances

The family camp committee should plan a budget so each family will know what the cost will be. It should be kept as low as possible, so each family who desires to participate may be able to do so. The committee will need to decide how to prorate the cost.

When families must prepare all of their own meals, they may be responsible to provide their own groceries, or there could be one purchasing group and a common commissary.

Promotion

The family camp committee should take the responsibility for promoting the family camp, possibly coordinating this with the general camp promotion of the planning committee. Promotion should begin in the fall and early winter, because vacation time of families is involved. It may be wise to promote the first camp by personal interviews with those who have already displayed a flair for camping and who can give leadership in future camps. As the number of camps for a congregation is increased, promotion can be by general announcements in the church bulletin and in the newsletter, by attractive posters with pictures from a previous family camp, by slides and movies, and by personal appearances before family groups. The personal interview should continue.

Any standards (children within a particular age bracket, etc.) to be used in selecting the families should be made clear in the promotion. Care *must* be taken not to give the impression that the family camp is only for a select group and that other families in the congregation are not welcome. It would be better to have no family camp than to develop cliques within the fellowship of the church!

Registration

Since families must plan in advance if the whole family is to do things together, it is not asking too much that registrations be in six to eight weeks before the camp. All registrations should go to the director-family, who acknowledges them and notifies families of their acceptance. Two or three families could be placed on a waiting list to take the place of dropouts.

A family portrait sheet should be filled out in detail for each family. See Appendix D, p. 109, for sample. This becomes the basis for grouping families, for determining what leadership can be expected from the group and what outside leadership is needed, and for sketching a framework of program possibilities.

A family health certificate is of great importance. It would be well to have the American Camping Association health certificates filled out for each member of the family. If this is not required, have the parents fill out a family health certificate and send it with the registration form. See Appendix E, p. 110, for sample. Particular attention must be given to limitations of activities, required medication, and special diets.

Program

As in all camping, everything that happens is program. Out of the happenings grow the "camptivities." The families or groups of families plan in order to meet their needs at this particular time in family life. Everything that is planned should be family-centered, although this does not mean that the whole family must do everything as a unit. They should, however, do as much as possible as a family.

1) meeting the necessities. There are tasks to be done at camp to serve the well-being of the group. Tables must be set, food served, and tables cleared. In some cases the food must be cooked and the dishes washed. The dining room, the lodge, the shelters, and the bathhouse must be cleaned. Wood must be cut and brought in for the fireplaces. These are community chores and should be shared by all the families. Assignments should be made so each will know its responsibility, and parents and children should share the tasks together. This can be work or recreation according to the attitude adopted.

There may be other tasks around the campsite which are for the good of others as well as of the family camp, such as repairing paths to prevent or decrease erosion, removing rocks, repairing walls, preparing for storage of the equipment which will not be used until next season, replenishing the wood supply at the small-group camp or at the lodge, and planting or working the garden where produce is grown for camp use. The manager can make other suggestions. Before you tackle a job, clear with the manager to be sure what you are planning is desired and that you will be doing it acceptably.

2) recreation. Recreation and fellowship are high on the list of priorities in family camping. This is vacation time, vacation time is for fun, and camping should be fun. Most recreation at home is in peer groups, because mother and father are working and only the children have time to play. Camp offers an excellent time for the family to play as a unit and to play with other family units.

Take this opportunity in the out-of-doors to do things that are different. Explore the woods and fields, climb the mountains, study growing things and animals, collect rocks and seedpods, enjoy swimming and learning to swim or to swim better, row, paddle, fish, discover constellations on a clear night, identify calls and sounds of nature, make things of materials gathered in the woods or fields or along the shore, construct useful things around the campsite (such as tables, seats around the campfire circle, and shelters and racks for different purposes), enjoy cookouts and snacks prepared over an open fire.

Plan games that are different from those at home, or adapt familiar games to the camp setting and make the equipment you will need. *Recreation in the Out-of-Doors* (see Resources, p. 140) will give you ideas. Some games of skill may not include all members of the family, so plan others to include all.

3) worship. Family camp is an ideal time for the family to renew its plans for family worship. There is time to read and discuss a portion of Scripture daily and to pray together. The reading of one of the Psalms before or after a study of the stars or of the story of creation at another appropriate time may be most impressive to adults as well as to children. Evening activities should not so compete with bedtime as to prevent serious talk and prayers in family units.

Evening worship might be planned for all of the families, or by separate families. There is no need to bring the usual trappings of worship out-of-doors. An informal service that is family planned and led—a short passage of Scripture, a few words fitly spoken, a familiar hymn softly sung, and a period of silence—may be all that is needed.

Devotional materials other than those families are accustomed to use should be made available during camp.

4) study. Study at camp? Yes, but not in the same way one would study in the classroom. For instance, when a family plans to lead other families in worship, there is study of the meaning of worship and what will be shared with the group. On Sunday morning a suitable passage of Scripture could be studied in the family group.

Research on a simple scale can be undertaken in many fields of nature, as families make discoveries and seek to know more about their finds. Study may be necessary in attempting some crafts or in making things for the camp area. Study may be listening to someone explain something, or watching a demonstration of something you want to learn.

The youth and adults might find time to read and discuss an article or even a book that is particularly appropriate. There could be a well-planned period of late-evening discussion when the younger children have gone to bed.

Study is different in camp, and it can be much fun. But do not try to force study on the group, or it will be ineffective.

5) relaxing. One sure thing a family camp should offer is a pace that is relaxed. It is not necessary to sit up late to watch a TV program or to play cards. Campers should try going to bed early and listening to the night sounds of nature, or to the patter of rain on the canvas shelter. It is not necessary to rush anywhere. They can listen to what children want to say, take time for family devotions, share the simple housekeeping jobs. There is time to think about things often pushed back in the mind, to enjoy the companionship of the family, and to enjoy the fun and fellowship of other families.

6) evaluation. The director should make careful plans for an evaluation of the camp in order to make recommendations to the family camp committee and to the overall planning committee. Specific questions should be presented for each family to answer, similar to those found on page 130. They should be given a chance to add comments not brought forth by the director's questions. The staff, particularly where there are leader-families, should give evaluations of their roles and reactions to camper participation, and then they should meet as a group to discuss what they feel happened to families.

The director should compile the written evaluations from families and staff in presenting his report to the family camp committee. He should always keep in mind future family camps and recommend families who can give leadership.

CHAPTER 4
LEADERSHIP

The main person in the camp is the camper. It is for him that the camp has been established. Therefore, it is the responsibility of the entire staff to know him and his needs; to help him to know himself and his needs; and to help him prepare himself, through the life of the camp, to live faithfully and cooperatively with others as he with more profound understanding accepts his role as a child of God involved in the mission of the church.

Staff members are chosen for their ability to help fulfill this task. Each must know himself to be a child of God doing the mission of the church now. He must know what his particular job is in this situation, how best to do it, and how he fits into the work of the total staff. He must recognize the lasting influence he may have in the lives of some or all of the campers, and of his fellow staff members as well.

The planning committee has responsibility for choosing the staff, although it usually designates a subcommittee on leadership selection and training to carry the load. This manual will continue to speak of these matters in terms of the planning committee, for the whole committee should feel a keen responsibility to help in every way possible to enlist the best staff available and to provide for them the training needed to accomplish their tasks.

Staff requirements will differ according to the program goals, the number of campers in a camp, and the number of camps operating at the same time. In order for each member to know his role and responsibilities he should have a written job description. He also should have access to the job descriptions of other staff members, so that he knows his relationship to them and knows that all needs will be cared for.

In addition to knowing as much as possible about the psychological and sociological traits of the camper, as was stated in the opening paragraph of this chapter, there are three basic qualifications for every staff person: Christian commitment, a love for persons and particularly for the age group with which he will work intimately, and a love for the out-of-doors. Each staff member should understand and accept the philosophy and objective of camping in Christian education. (A statement of philosophy might well be written into each job description.) Volunteer leaders will do much of their learning as they lead, provided they have this basic commitment. Every staff person must feel concern for every other person in the camp, whether he works directly with him or not, because the whole group is the family of God in this place and he wants each to have opportunity for Christian growth. Choosing persons with these characteristics is a great responsibility.

Each planning committee needs to write its own job description to fit its particular situation. Suggestions are offered here in two categories because more can be expected of permanent staff than of volunteer staff. The permanent staff are those employed for a summer camping season or for the whole year. The volunteer staff serve for a week or more, but they ordinarily do not receive remuneration for services rendered. The job descriptions might follow this form:

    I. Position:
    II. Responsible to:
    III. Has responsibility over:

IV. Responsibilities:
    A. General
    B. Specific
V. Qualifications needed:
    A. General
    B. Specific

To avoid conflicts, the planning committee needs to say clearly who carries what specific responsibilities in the camp organization. Each staff person can function better if he knows where to go with his needs and whose needs he is responsible to try to meet. This is particularly necessary when there are both permanent and volunteer staff members. There will be no attempt to spell this out in detail here, however, because of the variety of patterns in church camps.

The following list indicates jobs that are to be done; responsibilities may be combined or divided. The job description should not become a static thing. Each person should be asked after camp to evaluate his job description. Was it realistic? Was it a challenge or a burden? How could it be made more helpful? The planning committee should study these evaluations and rewrite job descriptions as necessary.

POSSIBLE JOB DESCRIPTIONS

PERMANENT STAFF

DIRECTOR

Responsibilities:

    Serves as advisory member of planning committee
    Is public relations agent for camping to sponsoring unit
    Is public relations agent to neighbors and community
    Recommends site development and expansion
    Serves on interdenominational and secular agency committees
    Represents the planning committee in American Camping Association and other professional camping groups
    Supervises the sponsoring unit office on camping
    Plans and supervises registrations
    Helps set up and supervises the bookkeeping
    Plans for and supervises promotion
    Keeps year-round contacts with campers and their families
    Helps keep files on leaders up-to-date
    Supervises keeping health files up-to-date
    Keeps accurate records of his work

Gathers camp records and evaluations and keeps them up-to-date

Assists planning committee in selecting volunteer directors and staff

Interviews and employs all permanent (paid) staff, in consultation with planning committee

Supervises and serves as counselor to the paid staff

Sets up training events for and with directors

Serves as counselor and advisor to volunteer directors

Represents the planning committee before government agencies—health department, farm bureau, conservation department, etc.

Studies to keep abreast of all phases of camping

Strives continually to raise camp standards

Serves as host to groups who visit or use the camp facilities

Keeps close watch on all contracts affecting the camp

Reports to the planning committee at stated times and makes full annual report

Conducts or attends closing evaluation session of each camp

Qualifications:

Is trained in field of Christian education and, if possible, in group dynamics

Has knowledge of, training in, and love for camping

Shows mature judgment and stability of character

Has demonstrated administrative skill

Is able to meet and make presentations before groups

Likes to work with people of all ages, singly and in groups

Has ability to lead and inspire leadership in camping

MANAGER

Responsibilities:

Works under the direction of the permanent director, or, if there is none, under the planning committee

Keeps abreast of camping through study and attending workshops and training events

Supervises the grounds crew, to see that the grounds and woods are kept in good condition

Keeps good relations with area fire warden, soil conservationist, and health officer

Supervises the garden when there is one

Supervises the maintenance of buildings and facilities, making all repairs he can

Purchases equipment and supplies as directed and keeps detailed account of spending

Keeps detailed record of repairs on equipment

Supervises the kitchen operation, unless someone else is designated to do so

Assists the dietitian in food purchases and storage

Sees that regular checks are made on water purity and health standards

Works with volunteer camp directors as a member of the staff

Serves as resource leader in leadership training and with small groups as skills and time warrant

Keeps small-group equipment in repair and supplies on hand

Attends closing evaluation session of each camp

Stores or supervises the storing of equipment and supplies in good condition and in order at the end of the camping season, making a careful inventory which he reports to the director or planning committee

Meets with the planning committee when invited

Makes provision for protection of property when no program is scheduled

Checks all buildings and facilities after each camp session

Has authority to deal with unauthorized persons on the grounds

Keeps the director or planning committee informed of needs

Qualifications:

Has administrative and purchasing experience and ability

Likes to work with persons of all ages

Displays diplomacy in dealing with people

Has practical skill in working with necessary farm implements and tools, in carpentry, and in painting

Shows knowledge of conservation practices

Practices good camping principles

CAMP SECRETARY

Responsibilities:

Works under supervision of the director (or manager)

Relieves supervisor of as many details as possible

Qualifications:

Has skills in typing, composing letters, filing, and simple bookkeeping

Meets people easily and makes them feel at home in her presence

Understands children and youth and tries to answer their questions patiently and creatively

Is able to carry on her work despite many interruptions and some confusion

Is not afraid to carry assigned responsibility

DIETITIAN

Responsibilities:

Works under supervision of the camp director (or manager)

Works with supervisor in preparing job descriptions for the kitchen staff

Works with supervisor in employing food handling staff

Sees that all food handling staff have health examinations

Attends pre-camp training and orientation if at all possible

Supervises or serves as dining room hostess

If there is no hostess, assists and supervises table setters and sweepers

Works with the grounds staff for efficient garbage disposal

Is responsible for planning and supervising all meals served in and from the dining room

Is responsible for purchase and storage of all foods

Checks all food deliveries; approves bills for payment

Studies opportunities to secure surplus foods, and makes applications

Keeps close accounting on food budget to practice economy, but does not sacrifice food service on the altar of economy

Checks with health counselor for special diets and allergies of staff and campers

Checks all cookout orders; suggests additions, deletions, or substitutions when necessary; does not make changes without consultation

Cooperates with health counselor on meals served to sick persons

Serves as resource leader to small groups when time permits

Joins small groups for cookouts when time permits

Sees that sanitation laws for handling and serving foods are followed

Makes complete inventory of equipment, supplies, and food at the end of camping season

Sees that kitchen, equipment, and storage room are in good condition for winter closing

Attends closing evaluation session of camps

Recommends purchase of canned goods and staples during year when substantial savings are possible

Qualifications:

Meets health standards

Has degree in home economics or its equivalent in experience, and has practical ability in handling and serving foods

Has purchasing, administrative, and supervisory ability

Is flexible enough to meet changing situations of a camp

Understands food tastes and needs of different ages

Is willing to help with the cooking when necessary

COOK

Responsibilities:

Works under the supervision of the dietitian

Prepares food for table service or thermal unit service. (There may be several cooks, each with specific food preparation responsibilities, such as baker, salad maker, etc.)

Serves the dishes to be taken to the table

Stores leftover, usable food according to directions

Keeps refrigerators in order

Keeps storerooms in order, if no one else assigned to do so

Keeps kitchen equipment, pots, pans, and counters clean and in order

Qualifications:

Meets health standards

Has experience in cooking for large groups

Has a cheerful disposition

Is flexible enough to meet new situations

Can adjust to children's needs as well as to adults'

Works well under supervision

Works well on a team in the kitchen

DISHWASHER

Responsibilities:

Works under the supervision of the dietitian

Receives dishes at counter and scrapes or rinses them

Operates the dishwasher efficiently

Stores dishes properly for next table setting

Puts garbage pails at proper place

Keeps storeroom in order
Helps fill cookout orders
Keeps kitchen and pantry floors mopped and clean
Accepts other jobs around kitchen and dining room as designated

Qualifications:

Meets health standards
Has a cheerful disposition and is a willing worker
Is flexible enough to meet various situations
Works well under supervision but does not need constant attention
Works well on a team in the kitchen

HEALTH COUNSELOR (**registered nurse**)

Responsibilities:

Works under the supervision of the permanent director (or manager)
Studies *The Camp Nurse* (see Resources)
Attends pre-camp training and orientation if time permits
Works closely with camp doctor in all ways, particularly in cases
   of insect sting or poisonous snakebite
Gets health center ready for opening of camp
Sees that all first aid kits are ready for use
Establishes with director a daily schedule for visits at health center
Purchases all medical supplies needed during camp
Always leaves note as to where she may be found when away from
   health center
Sees that registered first-aider is on call when she must be away
Posts numbers for emergency calls on health center door
Keeps emergency car available with keys handy
Keeps health center clean, orderly, and attractive
Receives health certificates from staff and campers when they arrive
   and checks them at once, noting needs for medication and diet,
   allergies, and limitations of activities; reports these to the small-
   group leaders
Reports special diets and allergies to the dietitian
Receives all medicines brought to camp and administers them ac-
   cording to directions
Reports significant information to small-group leaders
Attends all sick persons in health center or in shelter
Advises director when parents should be called
Administers medicines according to professional standards

Keeps accurate written records on all sickness and on medicines administered

Accompanies patients to doctor or hospital, unless detained by another patient; then sees that a competent adult accompanies the patient

Checks bathhouses daily for sanitation and health conditions and reports to director needs she finds. Checks to see that disinfectants are properly used

Serves as a resource leader to small groups as time permits

Leaves health center in order at close of camp. Returns medicines to campers. Discards any supplies that will not be usable by next camp

Makes inventory of condition of equipment and supplies and makes recommendations to the director

Turns over to the director all health certificates and records for safekeeping until the camper is twenty-four years of age, unless state statute of limitation is less. (This is most important in case of future legal suits.)

Participates in closing evaluating sessions

Qualifications:

Registered nurse, licensed to practice in the state

Can carry on functions in camp setting, sometimes with more limited facilities than she is used to

Is flexible enough to meet camp situations calmly

WATERFRONT DIRECTOR AND/OR LIFEGUARD

Responsibilities:

Works under the supervision of the permanent director (or manager)

Attends pre-camp training sessions if time permits

Is present for training period immediately before opening of camp

Checks all aquatic equipment

Establishes rules for aquatic area if none exist

Sees that swimming areas are properly marked

Discusses rules with staff to seek their cooperation

Keeps pool clean and equipment in order

Directs aquatic activities at the lake and/or pool

Seeks assistance from other staff when needed

Gives full attention to his lifeguarding duty when on duty

Tests swimming ability of staff and campers and indicates their limitations in the aquatic program

Strives to have every person in camp learn to swim or improve his swimming

Permits no dangerous horseplay in swimming

Directs use of buddy system in swimming, particularly in lake or open stream

Directs the boating, canoeing, and sailing program

Teaches safety rules in use of the types of boats available and insists on observance of them

Accepts other responsibilities assigned him that do not interfere with aquatic duties

Reports to director breakage and damage to equipment. Assists in repairs where possible

Makes complete inventory at end of camp and checks in all aquatic equipment

Participates in closing evaluation sessions

Qualifications:

Is at least 21 years of age and mature in judgment

Has had previous experience as lifeguard

Holds a Red Cross Water Safety Instructor's Certificate or its equivalent from organization having comparable standards

Understands the objectives and goals of church camping

Is clear in explaining the rules, firm in enforcing them, and has ability to make persons want to keep them

Has the ability to teach and is teachable himself

VOLUNTEER STAFF

THE DIRECTOR OF A CAMP SESSION

Responsibilities:

Works under the direction of the planning committee (or the permanent director)

Works with the various subcommittees of the planning committee to understand his role and to help them help him with the camp

Works with the leadership committee in selecting his staff, including resource persons

Keeps his assistant director informed on all plans and involves him when possible

Works with the program committee in selecting leaders' guides, resource materials, and library books

Is willing to take time for special study and training

Plans training for his own staff and directs their training

Assists in promoting camp through talks, brochures, and correspondence

Sets up plans for registering the campers if no central registering plan is in effect

Receives and acknowledges all applications, and informs campers of special rules to be observed, clothing to be brought, and personal equipment needed, plus the telephone number, mailing address, and the opening and closing hours of camp

Confers with his staff personally (if possible) about study materials before the first staff meeting

Seeks to weld a group of individual leaders into a harmoniously working community

Orients his staff to the site and responsibilities, so each will feel at home before the campers arrive

Pairs the small-group leaders into working teams

Groups the campers and small-group leaders for best working relationships

Greets campers and parents on opening day; helps the campers feel at home; seeks to make parents satisfied

Presides over or arranges to have someone else preside over all total camp meetings

Conducts staff meetings during camp as he feels they are necessary

Serves as the administrator of the camp, but uses democratic principles

Works with the permanent staff in such a way that all feel that they are one team

Is a counselor to the small-group leaders and other staff

Is available to the campers but does not interfere with the small groups

Is willing to be lonely during camp because he has trained his staff so well that he is not needed constantly (but keeps himself available)

Plans his evaluation program so that a daily review is taking place which can be evaluated later in the light of succeeding events

Conducts the final evaluation session

Writes notes of thanks to the staff and to the churches from which they come

Keeps clear records of his work from the time he becomes director until he makes a final report

Completes the report as soon as possible after the close of the camp and turns it in to the planning committee

Qualifications:

Is at least 25 years of age, but preferably older

Has time in his schedule for much pre-camp work, for pre-camp training, for the camp itself, and for follow-up

Has administrative ability in dealing with people, correspondence, promotion, and record keeping

Is well organized; can plan and carry out plans

Has had experience in church camping as a small-group leader

Has skill and ability to lead his staff in camp training

Understands and practices good methods in group work

Is able to supervise, but at the same time puts persons at ease.

Understands and has experience working with the age group of his camp

Is able to evaluate situations fairly

ASSISTANT DIRECTOR

Responsibilities:

Works under supervision of the director

Relieves the director by accepting assigned responsibilities

Is prepared to take over the director's role in case the director is unable to continue

Serves in some additional capacity in the camp, such as business manager, resource person, or small-group leader, as qualified and as the director may desire

Participates in closing evaluation session

Qualifications:

The same as for director, although he may not have had as much camping leadership

BUSINESS MANAGER *(may not be necessary in all camps)*

Responsibilities:

Works under directions of the director and with the finance committee as the director's representative

Prepares budget for the camp

Works with the public relations committee on preparation and distribution of posters and brochures

Sets up the registration procedure in consultation with director, handles registrations as they arrive, and assists the director in sending letters to campers and parents

Registers campers on opening day and receives fees, if they have not been sent in advance

Serves as liaison with camp management if the campsite is rented

Serves as liaison with community as need arises

Helps prepare lists of supplies and equipment needed

Serves as purchasing agent for camp—equipment, supplies, and food where necessary

Assists in preparing job descriptions for staff that he employs—cooks, dishwashers, etc.

Attends pre-camp training, serving as business manager, and participates in the training in every way possible

Has sufficient supply of food order, menu, and check-out blanks on hand

Checks out tools and equipment if no other plans have been devised

Checks all bills and expense accounts and pays them or authorizes their payment

Compiles detailed financial and statistical reports at close of camp for the director

Participates in closing evaluation session

Makes inventory of supplies and equipment at close of camp and sees that they are properly stored away

Qualifications:

Is mature in his judgment and systematic in handling matters

Is good at detail work

Recognizes his Christian stewardship for finances and materials

Is a good puchasing agent

Works well with people

SMALL-GROUP LEADERS

Responsibilities:

Works under supervision of the director

Is at least 19, and has had two years of college or its equivalent

Understands and practices good methods in group work

Studies materials and gathers resources that might help at camp

Attends all pre-camp meetings and training camps

Seeks to improve his camping skills by attending training opportunities other than those for his particular camp

Gives aid to less experienced staff when possible

Plans with co-leader as soon as they are paired

Writes or calls his shelter group if names are given him before camp

Learns as much about his campers as possible before camp

Comes to camp rested and ready for his task

Shares leadership role with co-leader and campers

Serves as counselor for his small group

Plans thoroughly but with flexibility for the first 24 hours

Greets campers and parents on arrival and helps campers settle in

Practices democratic principles in the group in reaching decisions; is not domineering

Leads campers to understand and use democratic principles in reaching decisions

Leads in daily review without making it an autopsy

Keeps systematic, worthwhile records on all his campers

Attends staff meetings

Reports to director matters he cannot handle

Helps campers check out supplies and equipment as needed and checks them in at close of camp. Reports those needing repairs

Fills out reports and evaluation sheets

Attends closing evaluation session

Writes campers and their parents at the close of camp

Has follow-up contact with campers during year if possible

Qualifications:

Understands the age group with which he is to work and has had some experience working with them

Understands Bible study and is able to help campers search for its truths

Is willing to give himself to the complete camp experience

Has sufficient camp skills and ability to adapt to situations and feel at home in camp

Is able to work with persons as a team member

Has the ability to inspire persons to bring out the best in them

Seeks to handle discipline by getting to the root of the problem; is willing to take time to do this

Does not show strong partialities

Is flexible and can adjust to change, though it may mean giving up his own pet project

RESOURCE PERSON

Responsibilities:

Is willing to spend the entire time at camp or has a clear understanding with the director about time he will be present

Becomes familiar with philosophy of the camp

Reads the leader's guide and other resource material to be aware of the theme and thrust

Participates in the pre-camp training. (This may be his place of service rather than during the camp.)

Is present at camp with staff before campers arrive

Is ready when needed

Participates in total camp program as nearly as possible

Is prepared not to be called on by all small groups, or for all of his time

Prepares report and evaluation on his work for the director

Participates in closing evaluation session

Qualifications:

Is competent in his own field or fields

Knows how to work with the age group; knows when to change the subject or to stop

Is skilled in sharing his knowledge and skills

Is at home in the camp setting

RECRUITING

WHOSE RESPONSIBILITY?

Some people feel that it is the responsibility of the leadership sub-committee of the planning committee to recruit the staff and thus relieve the director of many hours (or days) of work. Others feel that every director should enlist his own staff, to be sure he has persons with whom he can work harmoniously. Recruiting might best be a joint venture of the committee and the director.

If the director is a full-time employee of the sponsoring unit, his job description will allow time for correspondence and for traveling for personal interviews. In such a case, he will do most of the recruiting, keeping in close touch with the leadership committee. If he is a volunteer director who has another full-time position, he will need more help from the committee; the members should do some of the traveling and interviewing, in consultation with him. It saves time and money for members of the committee and the director to make up a list of potential leaders and divide the names, so those nearest can interview them. But even then, the one who can make the best appeal to an individual should do the interviewing, though it may mean more travel.

WHO IS RECRUITED?

The late Hedley S. Dimock, dean of George Williams College of Chicago, makes these pointed statements about the staff: "They are the 'spiritual' center of the camp community, the 'value center' of the camp in operation, the center for determining the 'educational destiny' of the camp, the chief center of satisfaction or frustration for both campers and staff personnel, the center of motivation for the growth of its members in competence, and, in summary, the morale center of the camp."[6]

Keeping these statements in mind, the planning committee should establish a personnel policy for each type of camp it conducts. A family camp will call for different personnel than a junior high camp; a camp for sixth-graders will need a different staff than a youth work camp; a completely decentralized camp will need one type staff, while a conference will need another.

Factors that help determine the personnel policy are minimum age, Christian profession, job qualifications and responsibilities, camping standards, and compensation. The personnel policy should be steadily improved through the years; it should be in writing to guide new committee members and new directors.

Who is recruited? Persons who are recognized as embodying the principles stated by Hedley Dimock, regardless of their positions in the community. One of the great thrills of the author was to see a New York City policeman and his wife serving as small-group leaders with sixth-grade boys and girls, and to see a university professor directing a camp of seventh-graders. Too long has church camping depended on ministers and directors of Christian education. The witness of lay men and women in camp can be very effective.

Seek leaders among those who like family camping, who like hunting and fishing, who like gardening and nature study, who are geologists and ecologists. Interview those who are trained to serve in youth character building organizations; help them see that their church needs their service and witness. Appeal to married couples who have no children, to those whose children are old enough to attend camp or are grown, and to those who can make provision to have their children cared for during the period of camp. Seek leadership from church school and public school teachers, from college and university professors. Ask the policeman, the government worker, the businessman. Older college students and graduate students are the largest staff pool at present. Continue to enlist ministers and their wives and directors of Christian education.

WHEN ARE STAFF RECRUITED?

All directors should be recruited by the last of October and all other staff by the middle of January. This does not mean that they cannot be recruited much earlier. Some will doubtless have to be recruited later, but much of this can be avoided if several extra leaders are on standby in case they are needed.

If the leadership committee is diligent and wise, it will be preparing leaders for years ahead. A director might understand that he will serve for three years, unless there is reason for him to serve a shorter term. He should be preparing someone to succeed him by having a person designated as his assistant each year. His assistant in his last year normally will become the next director. In this way there will be continuity in program, yet opportunity for change. The director can grow in his understanding of the job that is his.

The director can be choosing staff two and three years ahead of the camp as he trains and evaluates those with whom he works. At the close of one camp, he can issue tentative invitations for the coming year if the leadership committee approves such a policy.

When the committee finds it necessary to select the director in the fall, it should soon thereafter go over with him the recruitment policies and make a list of potential leaders. Invitations should then be issued.

HOW ARE THE STAFF RECRUITED?

When someone comes up with the perfect solution to staff recruitment, he will be immortalized in prose and poetry. There is no easy way, and the process is a long one. The best way known today is through personal interview by the director, particularly if he does not know the person. This gives each a chance to see and question the other. Philosophy and objectives should be discussed. Everything that is expected of the leader in time and commitment should be spelled out. It is possible that at the first meeting the prospective leader can make no firm decision because schedules and other matters must be cleared; he may need to consider his philosophy of camping as over against that of the director to be sure they can work harmoniously on the same team.

Another method of recruitment is to send a member of the leadership committee or another staff member for the interview. It is assumed that the person doing the interviewing is in agreement with the philosophy of the director and that he is representing him. This interview might be preceded by a letter from the director, stating that the person is to call and that he hopes he will give every consideration to the request. A letter from the director should follow the interview, stating clearly the name and location of the camp, the dates (including pre-camp training, orientation, and evaluation), advance preparation required, the size of the camp, and the size of the group with which he and his co-leader will work. There should be a written statement of philosophy and objective, along with the job description of what he is asked to do, if these were not presented in the interview. Whether he will receive an honorarium should be stated. Invite him to a specific meeting or make a definite appointment to discuss the matter further. Seek a reply by a definite date, allowing time to interview others if he cannot accept. Give him the facts he needs to make his decision so his will be a commitment to the whole program.

Another method of recruitment is through correspondence after recommendations have been thoroughly investigated. The information outlined above should be included in the letter.

HOW IS RECRUITMENT LIST MADE UP?

Records should be kept, in the sponsoring unit office, of staff members of previous years, of all who have ever been recommended, and of campers who might serve as staff when they are older. Pastors and other professional church workers should be alerted to make recommendations. Some planning committees require each church to recommend a leader for every five campers they plan to send to camp, and other churches are asked for recommendations even though sending fewer campers. Lists of church school leaders in particular age groups might reveal good leadership, and departmental superintendents might make recommendations. These are all recommendations only; the committee or the director must decide if the person will be asked to serve.

One sponsoring unit does training and recruiting all during the year by inviting couples to the camp for weekends. They camp and discuss the camping program. No commitments are sought for leadership for the coming season, but the camp director is able to appraise potential leadership.

TRAINING THE STAFF

The camp director must understand the objective and philosophy of Christian education in the out-of-doors and must see its potential in the total work of the church. The planning committee should make it possible for him to supplement his past training and experience by discovering opportunities for training, providing funds, and requesting from his supervisor release from his job to take training. Many city and state councils of churches plan interdenominational training camps and welcome leaders from outside their bounds. Denominations often plan training events especially for directors, and these are usually open to leaders from other denominations. Some colleges and universities offer special courses in night school dealing with camp administration, counselor training, human relations, and crafts. A director might set his own course of study if other opportunities are not available. He then needs to have the books provided. But it is better for him to work with persons who have had experience.

WHO TRAINS THE STAFF?

It is generally agreed that the director is responsible for training his own staff, but he will need the support of the leadership committee. The committee should set a tentative schedule of events according to their policy for leader training. It should discuss with the director his needs for resource persons to assist him and should provide honoraria for them. It must clear dates with the campsite and provide the necessary funds to pay expenses of staff to all training events. The schedule must be set in the fall in order to reserve the site and insure attendance of needed resource persons and staff.

WHAT SHOULD STAFF TRAINING INCLUDE?

Getting to know each other. The interview between the director and the staff person was the beginning of staff training. The two became persons to each other, rather than just names. It is necessary to extend this process to include the entire staff.

Getting to know the objective. Each has had an opportunity to study the objective on his own, but it may not have the same meaning for all the staff. An opportunity should be given to discuss it; after probing, testing, clarifying, and rephrasing, each staff member should rewrite it in his own words. Then he will ask himself, "Is my objective in harmony with that of the sponsoring unit?" More discussion may be necessary.

The philosophy of Christian education in the out-of-doors and the specific place of camping should become a part of the discussion on objectives. It will not be easy to work in harmony if there are wide differences of objective and philosophy. It may be better to replace staff.

Getting to know resources. The three greatest resources in camping are persons, the Scripture, and the natural order. We read in *Site Selection and Development:*

> So we invite you to plan with persons at the center of your concern in order that through leadership, facilities, and program the church may:
> 1. Relate man to God in his work of creation.
> 2. Teach man his responsibility for caring for God's gifts in the world of nature.
> 3. Interpret figures of Bible language and enrich many passages of the Scriptures.
> 4. Teach through the influence of living the gospel and discovering its meaning in personal relationships.
> 5. Relate persons to persons of peer groups in Christian community.
> 6. Relate mature Christians to less mature growing Christians.
> 7. Relate members of a family to each other meaningfully.
> 8. Relate families to other families and help persons reflect upon these relationships in the light of the gospel.
> 9. Put the meaning of Christian concepts into practice.
> 10. Use living situations for an extended period of study, worship, fellowship, and inspiration.
> 11. Provide for soul-searching renewal and program planning.
> 12. Provide an experience of personal acceptance by other Christians in the community.[7]

Do not lose sight of the fact that the campers are resources also. Study their personal records as soon as they are available and get to know them as persons as soon as possible.

Books are resources which you can get hold of early; see list starting on page 132. The leader's guide or resource book is a book of suggestions and thought starters. Encourage the staff to study it with this in mind; then the co-leaders can work out plans. The leader's guide may be put aside completely when they get to camp. At most, it will serve as an occasional reference book. The director should have available for each small-group leader or co-leader a basic book on camping skills, group work, and ecology. Reference books on nature study and outdoor cooking should be presented and discussed. These should be made available to the staff as they need them, before and during camp. The Bible is a basic book for leaders and campers. It is good to have different versions and translations on hand.

The site, facilities, equipment, and supplies are resources. Information about them must be given early, for camp plans must be made and suggestions in the leader's guide must be chosen, modified, or rejected according to the site, facilities, and equipment available.

Practice in skills. One usually thinks of camp skills in terms of hiking, identifying objects and creatures in nature, aquatic sports, construction of outdoor living facilites, cooking, arts, crafts using things from nature, the use of tools, the use of the compass, etc. He may forget the skill of Bible study in the camp setting, where he will deal with application of truth to life; the skill of group work in trying to understand why persons act and react as they do with certain individuals, and why different groups bring out different behavior; and skill in the use of democratic principles in reaching decisions which affect the life of the community as well as of individuals. All of these skills need to be learned and practiced.

Learning staff relations and responsibilities. These might be made clear by discussion, by a chart showing the organizational structure, and by a study of the different job descriptions. Staff relations will come clearer when they live in the setting where they are applicable.

Learning customs and procedures. Each camp has its own way of doing things and its own traditions, which may be supplemented by some procedures the director personally prefers. Each staff person needs to know the camp's table service and dishwashing procedure, and dining room standards, so that he can lead his campers into following them. He needs to know where equipment and supplies are kept, and the methods of checking them out and of returning them. Explanation of the menu and food order sheets for cookouts, when and how orders are to be placed and picked up, and the principles for sanitizing dishes and utensils and disposing of garbage in the small-group camps must be clear. The staff needs to know the recommended care of shelters, bathhouses and latrines, lanterns, etc., and the rules for cutting in the woods or getting fuel elsewhere. Gratuities are seldom given by parents in church camping, but the policy of dealing with any such gifts needs to be clearly understood.

Learning what records and evaluations are required. Staff must know what is required in the way of individual camper and group records, health records, cost accounting for cookouts and snacks, daily evaluations, and the final evaluation and report.

HOW SHOULD TRAINING BE CARRIED OUT?

Interviews and correspondence. Interviews and correspondence have been referred to as methods for recruitment. They are also a means of staff training. By them staff are introduced to the director and to the philosophy and objectives of the camp. An interview gives the director a chance to make his own appraisal of the person and to probe into his thought patterns as they discuss camping and this particular camp. Suggestions may be made that one or two of the basic books in camping be read.

In-town meetings. For day camping, in-town meetings may be all that are necessary, except for a visit to the site of the camp (which also may be in town). For resident camps, two or more in-town meetings should be planned. If distances make it difficult for all to gather in one place, the director may hold two or three gatherings in different towns, with him doing most of the traveling. These meetings may be held wherever there is enough room for the group to demonstrate and practice some of the camp skills.

The first in-town meeting should be held soon after the full staff has been enlisted, probably in February. This is a time for the group to get to know each other. It might be a supper and evening meeting, or just an evening meeting. Each person should identify himself and make a statement about his experience in camping and/or with the age group who will be in camp. Two or three favorite camp songs might be sung. This is the time for discussing the philosophy and objective, ending with each rewriting the objective in his own words. Slides or movies of the site might be shown to introduce new staff to the land and facilities. If each has already received the leader's guide and has had time to read it through, time should be given to discussing it. If it is to be given out at this meeting, then the director (or one he appoints) should give a quick run-through of the book to highlight important features for the group to discuss at the next meeting. After a discussion of the camp skills that will be needed, the director might assign specific skills for persons to work on before the next meeting, with the idea that they will demonstrate them and help others to practice them.

If the weather is not too cold, the meeting could move outside and close with a camp snack such as som'ores, mock angel food cake, and coffee made in a No. 10 tin can over an open fire. Each might be given a suitable stick from which to whittle his own coffee stirrer.

The second in-town meeting should be an all day or afternoon-evening affair held where the group can be outdoors to practice skills and cook a meal. If the weather is too cold for the evening meal, it can be the noon one, or the meal might be cooked over an open fireplace. Even though the director has planned the meal and has all of the ingredients and equipment ready, members of the group should fill out menu and food sheets and the equipment check-out sheet. Give them the menu and let them figure out what to order. Check and discuss the food sheets after the meal.

Sufficient time must be allotted to discuss the leader's guide and list program elements. Those who are familiar with the site might be able to elaborate on some of the suggestions. Time should also be devoted to a skill session. The director might bring a bundle of sticks or bamboo and a ball of binder twine for constructing a table, with a post or chair serving as a tree for anchoring one end of the table. The health counselor, the waterfront director, and the resource persons can outline what their plans are.

The third in-town meeting could be one in which co-leaders get together at their convenience to discuss the leader's guide, resource materials, group work, and camp skills. They should check on personal equipment and books which will enrich their activities and which are not furnished by the camp. The director must impress on them that they are planning *for* a program which will be built with the aid of the campers, not creating a program which they will impose on the campers.

Pre-camp training session. This is not a time for using free labor to get the campsite in order; it is staff training time! This meeting should be held at the campsite for two or three days. It should be held from three to five weeks before the opening of camp, unless one training session is held for the staffs of all the summer camps, in which case it may come more than five weeks before the opening of some camps. (Some directors prefer this session to precede camp immediately.) If the staff is paid and works the entire summer, it often includes many college students and teachers. Then the session might be held just before the opening of the first camp and last a week or longer, for probably their training has been limited to interview, correspondence, and reading.

If the camp training is for two days, it should begin as soon after breakfast as possible, or with an 8:30 breakfast served by the kitchen staff, and it should continue through the evening meal and evaluation the second day. The leaders should arrive the day before, settle in, and check to be sure everything is in order. If three days are available, the group could arrive in time to settle in before the noon meal and should remain until mid-afternoon the third day. This plan is preferable.

A framework of the period of time should be given, and then the groups should plan to fit into this pattern. The framework might be something like this: meals served in the dining room at 7:45 A.M., 12:30 P.M., and 5:45 P.M.; total group orientation first day at _____; evening snack in the dining room for those who wish to attend at _____; total group evaluation and closing session at _____.

The staff of a camp should function as a small group, living in the camp area with a small-group leader. If there are no more than twelve members on the staff, they may make up one small group with the director serving as the small-group leader. If there are more, then small groups of seven to ten members, each with small-group leaders, should be formed, and each director would serve as a resource leader for his groups.

After the total group orientation, each small group should take the framework and build its schedule for the training camp. Some groups will need to emphasize one thing more than the other. Time will prove to be too short to go into details about everything, but enough should be attempted to give each a sense of security. The following list will suggest things to be attempted in this training session:

Visit all facilities in the central area of camp
Plan for Bible study and private devotions
Have evening campfire for discussion, evaluation, and worship
Allow time for cleaning shelter and for personal habits
Clean the bathhouse and latrine. Learn the procedures to be used in the regular camp
Use the camp lanterns. Learn how they work and how to clean them
Eat in the dining room to learn customs of table setting, serving the tables, singing, dish washing, sweeping up, etc.
Have a rest period during the day
Browse through the library to see what is available
Cook one meal in the small-group camp. This will give practice in meal planning and ordering, checking out and returning equipment, cutting and gathering wood, planning the layout for the living area of the small-group camp, constructing a work table or sawbuck, learning fire safety in the woods, building the fire or fires necessary for cooking and for heating water for dish washing, improvising utensils out of tin cans, cooking and serving in the small-group camp, practicing dining etiquette in the woods; sanitizing dishes and disposing of garbage and trash, returning unused foods to the kitchen; and doing nature study as partici-

pants observe things growing around the site, listen to the birds, or prepare a centerpiece for the table. The first aid kit should be on hand

Explore as much of the campsite as possible for nature study opportunities

Seek the services of the resource persons: naturalist, waterfront director, craft director (if there is such a person), gardener, etc.

Take a short compass hike

Identify stars and constellations and listen for night calls and sounds

Set a realistic bedtime and keep it

Pre-camp orientation. Pre-camp orientation is the twenty-four hour period before the arrival of the campers. All members of the staff should be on hand and on time. Each person should have time to settle in—make his bed, unpack what he needs, and get into camp clothes. The director meets with the total group to explain last minute details and to give the information sheets on campers to the small-group leaders, if this has not been done. Questions affecting the whole group should be discussed at this time. Questions from individuals or from pairs of leaders should be discussed with them. Regulations regarding health and sanitation should be reviewed if necessary. Health certificates of all the leaders should be given to the health counselor, calling to her attention special needs and limitations. Make this meeting as businesslike as possible without rushing answers and decisions; then send the leaders off to continue their planning.

When the group comes in for meals, see that persons are designated to be host, serve, wash the dishes (if this is customary), and sweep. The director should be on hand all day to consult and counsel with staff persons who need him. He may assist the registrar in preparing to receive the campers, and should check on the library.

Staff meetings and counseling. Some directors plan for a staff meeting every day at a time which will interfere least with small-group plans. He may ask both small-group leaders to attend or he may ask one to represent them. Other directors feel that a staff meeting should be called only when there is an emergency. When one is held, the director should keep in mind that this also is staff training. He should be alert to his staff at all times, as he sees them coming and going around the central area or is invited to their small-group camps, and as he sees their campers. If they seem to have a problem, he should be available. If he feels that there is a problem and they have not sought him, then he should quietly make arrangements to see them. If he feels that one of the campers needs help, he should speak to the small-group leaders rather than to the camper, unless it is a matter of health or safety that requires immediate attention.

Evaluation and reports. When camp is over, leadership training has not stopped. The director may be called on to lead another camp, and many of the staff will be asked to serve again. It is time for records to be completed and evaluations to be made. Whether or not this makes for growth in leadership ability depends on the seriousness with which the director leads the group. This should be a time of soul-searching to evaluate successes and failures. It should not be just a wandering, general discussion.

It would be most helpful to the planning committee to have representatives from both the program and leadership subcommittees listening in or assisting in the evaluation session.

CHAPTER 5
PLANNING A YEAR'S WORK

Well run camps do not just happen; those that operate smoothly have had months of preparation. Everyone accepts this as true, but all too often no appropriate action is taken in the light of this fact. Planning for camps for the next year should begin for the planning committee and directors as soon as they have closed one year's camp season. They should get right to work to make out a schedule and decide in the light of it which members of the committee will accept which responsibilities. Although no two situations are identical, the following calendar may help the committee and directors plan for the year. It suggests when certain kinds of things need to be done and who might be asked to do them.

SEPTEMBER

THE PLANNING COMMITTEE

Organize for the work of the year.

Elect chairman if not designated by sponsoring unit.

Assign permanent and co-opt members to such subcommittees as are needed to carry the following responsibilities:

Site—

Supervise maintenance, operation, equipment, supplies, and volunteer work projects at own site; or the renting of suitable site.

Program—

Evaluate camps held.

Determine needs for next year and schedule camps.

Recommend program emphases.

Recommend leaders' guides and resource materials.

Check on year-round programs and schedules.

Leadership—

Recruit leaders.

Keep up-to-date records on leadership and job descriptions.

Plan training events.

Finance—

Plan budget and recommend fees.

Arrange and supervise handling of funds.

Audit accounts—always working closely with treasurer.

Public Relations—

Keep camping program before the churches.

Prepare reports to the sponsoring unit.

Keep good relations with the camp neighbors.

Prepare brochures and news articles on winter program.

Plan for and supervise registrations.

Write notes of thanks to directors and to their home churches.

Receive evaluations and prepare a report for the planning committee.

THE DIRECTORS OF PAST SUMMER

Complete evaluation reports; interpret to program subcommittee.

Write out recommendations for following year and send to program subcommittee.

Write notes of thanks to all staff members not already written, and encourage them to write their campers.

Send reports to denominational headquarters.

OCTOBER

THE PLANNING COMMITTEE

Site—

Check with program committee on needs for fall, winter, and spring events.

Check with manager on repair and replacement needs.

Check on storing of summer equipment and supplies so all will be in order. Make complete inventory. (This may be done in August or September in some areas.)

Program—

Review fall, winter, and spring events scheduled for campsite, and their needs.

Study statistical reports of camps in light of sponsoring unit's latest report.

Study evaluation reports from directors and make own evaluation of total program.

Begin determining program for next year and make tentative schedule for summer camps.

Assign study of new materials to committee members.

Inform leadership committee as to directors needed for next year.

Restudy and revise job descriptions.

Leadership—

Check on needs for fall, winter, and spring events.

Bring records of leadership up-to-date and begin engaging directors for next year.

Get training events dates to which leaders could be sent.

Set tentative dates for own pre-camp training events.

Finance—

Study finance records to date.

Begin budget preparation or adjustments that seem necessary.

Set fees for camp.

Public Relations—

Finish writing notes of thanks to directors and churches.

Plan ways of presenting camping to churches.

Prepare report to sponsoring unit.

THE DIRECTORS FOR NEXT SUMMER

Clear calendar for camp next year.

Confer on dates for leadership training events.

NOVEMBER

THE PLANNING COMMITTEE

Site—

Check to be sure that everything is properly stored for winter.

Work with manager to set schedule for building plans and repairs.

Meet with directors to go over site, equipment, and supplies.

Program—

Complete camp scheduling for next year.

Meet with directors to discuss and select guidance materials (leaders' guides).

Begin list of needed resource materials and library additions.

Leadership—

Complete the enlisting of directors.

Begin list of small-group and resource leaders for all camps.

Finance—

Keep other committees posted on financial status.

Public Relations—

Release advance information to churches on schedule and plans for next year.

Begin collecting data for, and make plans for summer brochure.

THE DIRECTORS

Meet with program committee and help select leaders' guides and resource materials.

Make recommendations for addition to the camp library.

Meet with leadership committee to make up list of camp leaders.

Clarify who will issue invitations to leaders. Start enlisting staff.

Meet with site committee to become familiar with site and equipment.

Present written request for equipment and supplies needed.

Study job descriptions of staff and suggest changes to strengthen leadership roles and ease tensions.

DECEMBER

THE PLANNING COMMITTEE

Site—

    See that the manager and his family and other permanent staff are remembered at Christmas.

    Clear camp schedule so manager will have some vacation.

Program—

    Chairman lays plans for January meeting.

    Send out letters to former campers after Christmas.

Leadership—

    Use college vacation to interview potential leaders.

Finance—

    Make preparation to have books closed and audited.

Public Relations—

    Consider camp alumni gathering with parents for a showing of camp movies and slides—maybe a preview of promotional pictures.

THE DIRECTORS

    Use college vacation to interview potential leaders.

    Remember former staff with Christmas letter.

JANUARY

THE PLANNING COMMITTEE

Site—

Keep contact with manager to help him in his needs.

Review schedule for the entire year.

Program—

Consider new events or expansion of the program in new areas.

Order leaders' guides and resource materials, and distribute them to the directors.

Prepare list of equipment and supplies for site committee.

Meet with directors to study leaders' guides and resource materials.

Plan with leadership committee for staff training sessions.

Leadership—

Confer with directors and complete leadership.

Plan with program committee for leadership training and for leadership for new events.

Renew contracts with permanent staff.

Finance—

Make report to sponsoring unit.

Check with all committees on financial needs.

Arrange for petty cash for the directors.

Public Relations—

Complete brochure and registration forms.

Mail posters and brochures to churches.

Arrange for mailing brochures to campers of past year or two.

Make up schedule of special presentations to groups in churches for next two months.

Complete plans for receiving and acknowledging registrations.

THE DIRECTORS

Confer with leadership committee and complete staff recruitment.

Distribute leaders' guides and resource materials.

Plan for get-acquainted and study session with leaders.

Get and distribute to staff the schedule of training events that are sponsored interdenominationally or by Red Cross, American Camping Association, school, or other community agencies, and make plans to participate in some of them. Encourage your staff to participate.

FEBRUARY

THE PLANNING COMMITTEE

Site—

Begin assembling equipment and supplies for pre-camp training.

Begin list of equipment and supplies for camps.

Check with specialists on site needs.

Program—

Work with leadership committee on staff training.

Leadership—

Fill vacancies that occur in staff.

Work with program and site committees and directors on staff training.

Engage special resource persons for staff training meetings.

Finances—

Work with manager and leadership committee on staff training.

Public Relations—

Continue promotion through churches.

Develop newspaper articles.

Plan for dinner meeting with camp neighbors in spring to discuss mutual concerns, cooperation, and the camp program.

Begin registering campers.

THE DIRECTORS

Work with leadership committee to complete staff.

Recommend special resource persons for staff training.

Hold first get-acquainted and staff training study session.

MARCH

Site—

Work with manager and program committee on foreseeable needs of summer.

Plan for necessary repairs to waterfront.

Program—

Confer with public library about setting up a lending library at camp.

Check on all order blanks needed for camp and revise them as necessary.

Check with planning committee to be sure camper and staff accident and health insurance are available.

Continue working with directors on staff training.

Finances—

Receive registration fees and check bookkeeping system.

Public Relations—

Continue promotion.

Continue registrations, sending information to directors.

THE DIRECTORS

Keep alert to the needs of your staff.

If staff meeting was not held in February, by all means hold get-acquainted and staff training session.

Help leadership committee fill vacancies.

APRIL

THE PLANNING COMMITTEE

Site—

Invite all camp staff to meeting at site or be host to staff training at site.

Check with manager on opening camp for summer.

Take inventory of condition and supply of equipment.

Program—

Assist directors in staff training.

Leadership—

Assist directors in staff training.

Finance—

Work with all committees on financial needs.

Public Relations—

Continue registrations.

Prepare newspaper article with pictures of staff training on site.

Consider pictures of staff-training for promotional materials for next year.

THE DIRECTORS

Recheck spring camp training events and attend with as many staff as possible.

Complete your plans and possibly conduct your pre-camp staff training on the site.

MAY

THE PLANNING COMMITTEE

Site—

> Have the health authorities inspect the site and give certificate for conducting camps.
>
> Correct areas where standards are not met.
>
> Prepare to have regular summer checks of drinking and recreational water supplies (unless this is done all through the year).
>
> Make sure the site is ready for the camps.

Program—

> Complete arrangements with public library for lending library at camp.
>
> Confer with directors on last-minute needs.
>
> Check on all program supplies to be sure everything is available in quantities needed.
>
> Discuss and plan for the fall and winter events.

Leadership—

> Assist directors in staff training.
>
> If possible, have on stand-by trained persons who can fill emergency vacancies on staffs.
>
> Recheck needs for fall and winter events.

Finances—

> Check with all committees to be sure needs are met.

Public Relations—

> Continue registrations, reporting regularly to the directors.
>
> Prepare for newspaper articles during camps.
>
> Prepare for promotional picture taking during camp.
>
> Consider plans for visits and tours of camp.
>
> Make plans to entertain neighbors during camp.

THE DIRECTORS

> Hold pre-camp training session on site, if not already held.
>
> Make co-counselor assignments if not already done. Study personal information sheets of campers and set up shelter groups.
>
> Meet with staff as necessary to give assistance.

JUNE-JULY-AUGUST

THE COMMITTEE

Site—

Keep in close touch with manager to assist him where there are needs.

Visit camp to observe, but do not interfere with the shelter and small groups.

Program—

Provide the directors with evaluation blanks for their staffs and for themselves (different blanks).

Stand ready to assist the directors when called upon.

Visit camp to observe.

Leadership—

Stand ready to assist the directors and to fill vacancies.

Visit camp to observe.

Finance—

Keep regular check on income and expenditures.

Pay all bills and salaries promptly.

THE DIRECTORS

Set up and direct the pre-camp orientation and training for 24 to 48 hours immediately preceding camp.

Serve as host to greet campers and to meet parents.

Be a counselor to your staff.

Serve as liaison person for your staff and the permanent staff.

Serve as a resource leader when called upon.

Keep records for your camp.

Check the camp for cleanliness and for clothing and articles left; report broken or lost equipment.

Conduct the post-camp evaluation session.

Make petty cash account report.

Prepare and mail in reports as soon after camp as possible.

Write notes of thanks to your staff (or their families) and to the church from which they came.

APPENDICES

A. Application for Camp Staff Position
B. Sample Registration Blank
C. Information from Camp Registrant
D. Family Portrait Sheet
E. Family Camp Health Report
F. Camp Employee Health Examination Form
G. Camp Health Examination Form (Children, Youth, and Adults)
H. Camp Health Record
I. Food Service Plan for Dining Lodge
J. Menus and Food Orders
K. Table of Weights and Measures and Approximate Servings
L. Equipment Request
M. Proposed Camp Budget
   Church Camp Comparative Statement of Income and Expense
   Church Camp Statement of Assets and Liabilities
N. Abbreviated Selected Standards American Camping Association
O. Staff Evaluation of Camp
P. Director's Counselor Evaluation Sheet

104

APPENDIX A

Please enclose small photo

APPLICATION FOR CAMP STAFF POSITION

Date _____

Name _____ Age _____ Date of birth _____

Home Address _____ Telephone _____

School Address _____ Telephone _____

Height ____ Weight ____ S.S. No. _____ No. exemptions claimed ____

Schools attended: Major: Year graduated:

_____   _____   _____

_____   _____   _____

_____   _____   _____

_____   _____   _____

Local Church Affiliation _____
What is your vocation (or intended vocation)? _____

Camping experience:
As camper___ Number of seasons _____ As Counselor___ Number of seasons _____
Where _____
What specific responsibilities have you had as counselor? _____
_____
With what age groups have you worked in camp? _____
With what age group do you prefer working? _____
What experience have you had in campcraft? _____
        Outpost camping? ___ Hiking? ___ Overnight trips? ___ Travel camping? ___
Are you an American Red Cross First-aider? _____ Senior Life saver? _____
                    Water Safety Instructor? ____ Year Qualified ____
Have you done any group work with children or adults other than camping? _____
(Indicate kinds of work) _____
_____

What are your hobbies? _____

Camp activities: (Check **once** those with which you feel you could assist; check **twice** those you feel qualified to lead.)

Water Sports	Athletics	Nature Lore	Campcraft
Swimming Instruction	Volleyball	Woodcraft	Fire Building
Diving	Badminton	Stars	Axmanship
Rowing	Softball	Trees	Lashing
Canoeing	Horseshoes	Flowers	Overnight Hikes
Sailing	Archery	Birds	Trail Cookery
		Others	"Orienteering"

Special Activities	Music	Arts & Crafts
Folk Dancing	Lead Singing	Basketry
Square Dancing	Play and Instrument	Indian Lore
Photography	Accordian	Painting and Sketching
Group Games	Guitar	Weaving
Impromptu Dramatics	Piano	Nature Crafts
Worship	Other	Pottery and Molding
		Whittling

References: (List three with addresses)

1. _____

2. _____

3. _____

Date _____   _____

                                           Signature

APPENDIX B

REGISTRATION BLANK (Side 1)
Camp _____ (19_____)

M ( )
F ( )

Name _____
(Please print or write clearly)

Address _____
(street)

_____
(city)   (state)   (zip)

Date of Birth _____ School Grade May 1 _____
Have you previously attended camp? _____ Year (s) _____
Have you attended other church camps? _____ Year (s) _____
Signature of Parent or Guardian _____
Address (if different from above) _____
    Telephone: Home _____ Business _____

A registration fee of $_____ is required for each applicant
Mail to: Registrar (give address)

I would like to register for: ___
FIRST CHOICE

Camp _____ Date _____

SECOND CHOICE (in event first choice is filled)

Camp _____ Date _____

REGISTRATION BLANK (Side 2)
(to be filled out by pastor)

I recommend _____
who is ___ is not ___ a confirmed member of _____
(church)

and who attends Sunday school regularly_____ occasionally_____ not at all_____.
Remarks _____
Pastor's Signature _____
Church _____
Address _____

CHURCH PAYMENT CERTIFICATE
(to be filled out if church is paying part of tuition)

$_____ may be expected in payment for this camper from:
Church (or Sunday school) _____
Signed _____ Position _____
Address _____
Remarks _____

APPENDIX C

Return to: _____
by (date): _____

INFORMATION FROM CAMP REGISTRANT

M ( )

My name is _____ F ( ) School Grade (April)_____
My address _____
(street)   (town)   (state and zip)

My phone number _____My birth date _____
(month) (day) (year)

My parents' names _____
(father)   (mother)

If parents are separated, divorced, deceased, etc., please mention here _____
_____

My father's job is _____
My father works at _____
(name of firm)   (address)   (phone)

My mother works at _____
(name of firm)   (address)   (phone)

I have _____ brothers living at home, ages_____
I have _____ sisters living at home, ages _____
Names of grandparents or other relatives living in my home _____

I have ( ), do not have ( ) definite responsibilities at home. They are _____
_____

I receive a regular allowance: Yes ( ) No ( )
I usually go to bed at _____ o'clock. I usually get up at _____ o'clock.
I have never ( ), seldom ( ), often ( ) been away from home before.
I have attended other camps or conferences. They were:

(name)   (place)

I attend _____ in _____
(church)   (name of town)

My pastor's name is _____
I am ( ), am not ( ) a communicant member of the church.

My parents' activities in our church are _____

Activities I participate in in my church are_____

(name any offices you hold)

Activities I share in my school are _____

_____

(name any offices or responsibilities you hold)

Have you had a part-time job at any time? _____ What type of work? _____

_____

Do you have a job now? _____ What type of work? _____
I have the following talents and abilities: _____

_____

I play the following musical instruments: _____
I play the following sports: _____
I belong to the following clubs, teams, organizations: _____

_____

These are some of my hobbies: _____

_____

STATEMENT FROM THE PARENTS

I have read the above information and concur in it. I understand that this information is being requested since my son or daughter has registered for a summer camp
or conference. In addition I would share the following:

Signed _____

APPENDIX D

Please complete and return to: _____

FAMILY PORTRAIT SHEET

Names of Couple _____ and _____ _____
                          (husband)   (wife)   (surname)

Name of Other Adult _____ Nickname _____

Names of Children   Age Sex Grade Nickname

_____ ____ ____ ____ _____
_____ ____ ____ ____ _____
_____ ____ ____ ____ _____
_____ ____ ____ ____ _____

Father's Nickname _____Occupation _____
    Responsibility in church and community _____
    Hobbies or interests _____
Mother's Nickname _____ Occupation (formerly or now) _____
    Responsibility in church and community_____
    Hobbies or interests _____
This will be our _____ year in a family camp.

To help us get a clearer picture of your family's interests and skills, please check the following by writing names in the blank spaces:

	Like to Learn	Like to Participate	Can Lead
group singing			
dramatics			
folk dancing			
story telling			
nature study			
crafts (specify)			
sports/games			
aquatic activities (specify)			

(Use back of this sheet to identify others.)

Special Needs:
Dietary or medical _____
Allergy _____
Restriction on activity _____

APPENDIX E

FAMILY CAMP HEALTH REPORT*
(Fill out and bring to camp)

Family Name _____

Address _____

           (street)   (city)   (state and zip)

The director suggests the following **Family** health questions for your guidance and for the convenience of the camp nurse.

1. Does any member of the family have diabetes or any other disease requiring diet regulation or medication? Please list the name of the person and the disease.

2. Has any member of the family ever suffered from or been told they have a heart disease severe enough to limit their activities? Which one?

3. Do you now know that a member of your family will need medical attention while at camp? If so, state the condition and need.

4. Have you had tetanus shots within the last three years?

---

* This is to be used only if the camp policy does not require the entire family to go to their family doctor for a check-up before camp. Each family will take responsibility for the health and well-being of its members as if they were at home.

A better plan is to check for each person the first page of the appropriate blank which follows in the appendices.

CAMP EMPLOYEE HEALTH EXAMINATION FORM

DEVELOPED AND APPROVED BY

AMERICAN CAMPING ASSOCIATION and AMERICAN ACADEMY OF PEDIATRICS

```
┌─────────────────────────────────────┐
│                                     │
│                                     │
│                                     │
│            Camp Name                │
└─────────────────────────────────────┘
```

(This side to be filled in by employee—professional or maintenance)

Name_____ Birth Date_____ Age_____ Sex_____
      Last   First

Address_____

In case of emergency notify_____ Phone_____

     Address_____

HEALTH HISTORY:
I have had the following illnesses as checked. Any incurred within the last year are double checked:

Allergies: Asthma, Hay Fever	Colds_____ ____	
Exema, Others_____ ____	Discharging ear_____ ____	
Frequent Sore Throats_____ ____	Shortness of Breath____ ____	
Sinus Trouble_____ ____	Convulsive Seizures	
Headaches_____ ____	or Fainting Spells____ ____	
Goitre_____ ____	Night Sweats_____ ____	
Typhoid Fever_____ ____	Frequent Diarrhea_____ ____	
Tuberculosis_____ ____	Frequent Urination_____ ____	
Rheumatism_____ ____	Other illnesses_____ ____	
Chicken Pox_____ ____	_____ ____	
Mumps_____ ____	_____ ____	
Sleepwalking_____ ____	Operation_____ ____	

I have had the following immunizations as checked:

	Check	Date	Comment
Tetanus Toxoid	____	_____	_____
Typhoid Vaccine	____	_____	_____
Diphtheria Vaccine	____	_____	_____
Smallpox Vaccine	____	_____	_____
Others	____	_____	_____

Chest X-Ray by State or County T.B. Association is recommended before Physical Examination.

Special limitations or medication i.e. glasses must be worn continuously.

_____

To my knowledge I (have____) (have not____) been exposed to a contagious or infectious disease in the past three weeks.

Date:_____

                          _____
                             (STAFF MEMBER'S SIGNATURE)

OTHER SIDE TO BE FILLED OUT BY A LICENSED M.D. AFTER YOU HAVE COMPLETED THE ABOVE.

Form 104 - 54 2M American Camping Ass'n., 343 S. Dearborn St., Chicago 4, Illinois

PHYSICAL EXAMINATION - To be filled out by a Licensed M. D.

(Not sooner than one week prior to employee's arrival at camp)

The object of this examination is to determine that the employee:
1. Is physically fit to engage in strenuous activities without harm to himself.
2. Does not have any contagious or infectious condition that could be conveyed to others.

PHYSICAL EXAMINATION: Satisfactory   Unsatisfactory

Posture - General Nutrition _____

HEAD AND NECK:
    Eyes_____
    Ears_____
    Nose_____
    Throat - General Condition_____
    Teeth -- General Condition_____
    Tonsils_____

CHEST:
    Heart - General Condition_____
    Pulse Rhythm_____
    Blood Pressure_____

LUNGS:
    General Condition_____
    Chest X-ray_____

ABDOMEN:
    Tenderness - Organs palpable_____
    Hernia_____

EXTREMITIES:
    Deformities_____
    Veins_____

SKIN:
    General Condition_____
    Pediculosis_____
    Ringworm_____
    Athletes Foot_____

Hemoglobin_____ Urinalysis_____
Menstruation_____
Contra - Indications to Swimming_____
*Stool Culture_____*Throat Culture_____*Kahn Test_____*Vaginal Smear_____
Reactions to Penicillin or other drugs, etc._____
Advice regarding patient: (Full activity, restricted activity, no heavy lifting, etc.)
_____
_____

_____ M.D.
Examining Physician

Phone_____ Address_____

Date_____ _____

*State Health Regulations must be observed - especially for Kitchen Staff.

APPENDIX G

CAMP HEALTH EXAMINATION FORM
for CHILDREN, YOUTH and ADULTS
Developed by
AMERICAN CAMPING ASSOCIATION, INC.
in consultation with
The American Medical Association and The American Academy of Pediatrics

RETURN TO:

_____
(camp name)

This side to be filled in by parent or adult camper and checked with physician at time of examination.

Name_____ Birth Date _____ Sex _____ Age _____
　　　　Last　　　　　　First　　　　　Initial

Parent or Guardian (or Spouse) _____ Phone _____
　　　　　　　　　　　　　　　　　　　　　　　　　　　　　Area and Number

Home Address _____
　　　　　　　Street & Number　　　　　　　City　　　　　State　　　　Zip Code

If not available in an emergency notify:

1. _____ Phone _____
　　Name　　　　　　　　　　　　　　　　　　　　　　　　　　Area and Number

_____
　　　　Street & Number　　　　　　　City　　　　　State　　　　Zip Code

or　2. _____ Phone _____
　　　Name　　　　　　　　　　　　　　　　　　　　　　　　　　Area and Number

_____
　　　　Street & Number　　　　　　　City　　　　　State　　　　Zip Code

HEALTH HISTORY: (Check — giving approximate dates)

		Allergies		Diseases	
Ear Infections	_____	Hay Fever	_____	Chicken Pox	_____
Rheumatic Fever	_____	Ivy Poisoning, etc.	_____	Measles	_____
Convulsions	_____	Insect Stings	_____	German Measles	_____
Diabetes	_____	Penicillin	_____	Mumps	_____
Behavior	_____	Other Drugs	_____	Asthma	_____

Operations or Serious Injuries (Dates)_____

Chronic or Recurring Illness _____
_____

Other Diseases or Details of Above_____
_____
_____

Any specific activities to be encouraged? _____
　　　　　　　　　　　restricted? _____

IMPORTANT: *Please notify the camp if this camper is exposed to any communicable disease during the three weeks prior to camp attendance.*

Suggestions from Parents _____
_____
_____
_____
_____
_____
_____

AMERICAN CAMPING ASSOCIATION, INC.
Bradford Woods — Martinsville, Indiana　　　　(OVER)
12-67

PARENT'S AUTHORIZATION

This health history is correct so far as I know, and the person herein described has permission to engage in all prescribed camp activities, except as noted by me and the examining physician.

In the event I cannot be reached in an EMERGENCY I hereby give permission to the physician selected by the camp director to hospitalize, secure proper treatment for, and to order injection, anaesthesia or surgery for my child as named above.

Signature _____

Date _____

IMMUNIZATION HISTORY

Required immunizations must be determined locally. This is a record of dates of basic immunizations and most recent booster doses.

DTP Series _____ booster _____ Tetanus Booster _____

Polio OPV (Sabin)_____ booster _____ Typhoid _____

Measles Vaccine (live) _____ Tuberculin Test _____

German Measles (Rubella) _____ Mumps Vaccine (live)_____

Smallpox _____ Other_____

MEDICAL EXAMINATION — *To be filled out by licensed physician.*

This examination should be performed within six months of arrival at camp. Examination for some other purpose within this period is acceptable. Examination is for determining fitness to engage in strenuous activities.

Code: √ – *Satisfactory*
X – *Not Satisfactory (explain)*
0 – *Not Examined*

Hgt._____ Wt. _____ B. P. _____ Hgb. Test _____ Urinalysis _____

Eyes _____   Extremities _____

  glasses _____   Posture (Spine)_____

Ears_____   Skin_____

Nose _____   Allergy:

Throat _____   Please specify

Teeth _____   _____

Heart _____   _____

Lungs_____   General Appraisal:

Abdomen _____   _____

Hernia _____   _____

(For Girls and Women)
Has this person menstruated? _____   If not, has she been told about it? _____

If so, is her menstrual history normal? _____   Special considerations: _____

Recommendations and restrictions while in camp.

Special Diet_____

Special Medicine (name it) _____ Is parent sending it? _____

Swimming, diving_____

Strenuous activity_____

Other_____
_____
_____

I have examined the person herein described and have reviewed his health history. It is my opinion that he is physically able to engage in camp activities, except as noted above.

_____ M.D.
Examining Physician

Telephone_____   Address _____
  Area Code and Number

Date _____
_____
  Zip Code
(OVER)

APPENDIX H

CAMP HEALTH RECORD
(Individual—at Camp)

Developed and Approved by
American Camping Association and American Academy of Pediatrics

_____
Camp Name

Name _____ Age _____ Sex_____
Entrance Date _____ Departure Date _____

Examination   **Important Observations to Follow While at Camp**

	Entrance	Departure	
	By _____	By _____	
Height			
Weight			
Temperature			
Eyes			
Nose			
Ears			
Throat			
Teeth			
Posture			
Skin			
Feet			

Instructions and Report to Parents or Guardian: (Health Progress)

_____
_____
_____
_____

Signature _____

(Keep health record on other side)

Form 103-54 American Camping Association, Bradford Woods, Martinsville, Ind.

Camper's Name

(last)

(first)

(initial)

Cabin or Tent

APPENDIX I

FOOD SERVICE PLAN FOR DINING LODGE

Meal times offer prime opportunities for teaching-learning. In addition to being a time to satisfy our physical need, meals are times for fellowship, service, and appreciation of others. There is no one way for table service, because camps differ greatly in equipment and arrangement, but family style service offers much in helping campers—adults and youth—to learn. Round or square tables to seat eight persons are preferred. Serving dishes for eight should be standard equipment.

The principles of table service set forth here designate a leader to help everyone enjoy his food and the fellowship, give stability to a group, divide the work, save confusion, equalize the servings, eliminate waste, encourage conversation as a total group, and develop a sense of consideration for others. They help teach good table manners, which are often lacking in our cafeteria society.

I. Setting the Tables

1. The waiters report to the dining lodge 15 minutes before the meal to set the tables.
2. A sample setting and copy of the menu will be placed on a serving table, with a list of dishes and silverware needed on each table. In some cases, the kitchen staff will have the dishes and silverware for each table on a tray.
3. The waiters will clear and wash the tables before setting the places.
4. They will place condiments and cold foods on tables before the campers come in.

II. Serving the Meal

1. After the blessing, the waiters will bring the hot food from the kitchen and place it before the host.
2. The person designated host will sit at the head of the table and serve all plates, passing the first plate to the person on his right and continuing until all on right are served, and then passing plates to the left. He may ask the person on his right to help serve if there are four dishes.
3. The host should encourage each person to eat some of each food, but will give small or regular servings according to the eating habits of individuals.
4. All wait to begin eating until the host has completed serving everyone and picks up his fork to start.
5. The host is alert to the needs of everyone; he requests the waiter to go for refills when necessary; he divides the remaining food as equally as possible.
6. The waiter is also alert to needs of the group and may offer to go for refills of dishes and pitchers if the host has not recognized the need. Only the waiter brings refills.
7. The host, with clearance from the director, indicates when the group, or individuals in some cases, may leave the table.
8. The person seated opposite to the host pours beverages after the waiter has brought them in.
9. The waiter sits to the left of the host.
10. All individual dishes served by the waiter should be served from the left side, except beverages. A left-handed guest should have beverages served to his left. Plates may be removed from either side and the beverage holders from the right (unless the person is left-handed and has his cup and glass on that side).

III. *Clearing the Tables*

1. Dishes from the main course should be removed before serving the dessert. Take the serving dishes to the kitchen first, using a tray to carry them.
2. Remove one place setting at a time, beginning with the host, and continuing to the right. Scrape with a rubber scraper at the serving stand and stack on the tray. Do not overload the tray.
3. Empty ash trays and put napkins in box designated for them.
4. When everything has been removed from the table, the waiter sponges it with soapy water, catching crumbs in a napkin. This completes his job, unless he is expected to sweep the floor.

IV. *Announcements, Singing, Table Games*

1. After the tables have been cleared, the director or a designated person may make announcements, lead in the singing of a few songs, or direct a table game or two. No singing and antics during the meals.

V. *Sweeping the Dining Room*

1. If an insect spray is needed, the sweepers should spray the tables after everyone has left them.
2. The sweepers proceed to their duty, being careful to get all particles of food that have fallen on the chairs or the floor.

(Adapted from National Camp, Matamoras, Pennsylvania. Permission of the late Dr. L. B. Sharp.)

118

APPENDIX J

MENUS AND FOOD ORDERS
(Give to dietitian 24 hours before needed.
You may need to adjust the time limit.
Make duplicate copy to keep.)

Group _____ Number in Group _____
Date of Cookout _____ Guests _____
Order filled by: _____ Checked by: _____

MENU	SUPPLIES	COST
Breakfast	Meat and Dairy Products:	
	Fresh Vegetables and Fruit:	
Lunch		
	Canned Food:	
Dinner		
	Bakery Products:	
Snack		
	Staples:	

(Adapted from National Camp, Matamoras, Pennsylvania. Permission of the late Dr. L. B. Sharp.)

APPENDIX K

TABLE OF WEIGHTS AND MEASURES
APPROXIMATE SERVINGS

Suggested allowance for food per camper:
Breakfast _____
Lunch _____
Supper _____

Measures in Cans (allow ½ cup per serving)
#1 can = 1½ cups food
#2 can = 2½ cups food
#2½ can = 3½ cups food
       pear halves 8-10
       peach halves 8-10
       pineapple slices 8
       plums 8-10
3 or # 5 can = 5½-6 cups food
#10 can = 12-13 cups food

Measurements
3 teaspoons = 1 tablespoon
16 tablespoons = 1 cup
2 cups = 1 pint
2 pints = 1 quart
32 liquid ounces = 1 quart
1 cup pancake mix = 14 pancakes
box of Ralston = 3½ cups
8 oz. box cornflakes = 22 cups
1 sq. chocolate = 3 tbsp.

FOOD AND AMOUNT*	MEASURE	SERVES	COST
Apples—1 doz.	. . .	12	_____
Apples (dried)	5 cups	10	_____
Apricots (dried)	3 cups	6	_____
Bacon (med. strips)	30 slices	15 (2 slices)	_____
Bananas	3 average	. . .	_____
Beans (dried)	2 cups	12	_____
Beans (lima)	2 cups	12	_____
Beans (fresh)	. . .	4	_____
Beef (raw)	. . .	2–4 (if no bones)	_____
Beef (dried)	. . .	8 (in creamed sauce)	_____
Beef (ground)	2 cups	3–4 (in patties)	_____
Beets	. . .	5	_____
Bisquick—2 cups	2 cups	(12 biscuits or muffins)	_____
Bread—1 loaf	22–24 slices	. . .	_____
Butter	2 cups	. . .	_____
Cabbage	. . .	7–8 (salads); 4 (cooked)	_____
Carrots	. . .	8–11	_____
Cheese (American)	16 slices	16 (1 oz. servings)	_____
Cheese (cottage)	2 cups	6	_____
Chicken—1½-2 lbs.	1 whole	4	_____
Chocolate—1 oz.	1 square	. . .	_____
Cocoa—1 oz.	¼ cup	. . .	_____
Coconut	6 cups	. . .	_____
Coffee (ground)	5 cups	40–50	_____
Cornflakes—¼ lb.	11 cups	10–11	_____
Cornmeal	3 cups	. . .	_____
Corn syrup—¾ lb.	1 cup	. . .	_____

* Unless otherwise indicated the amount of food used is 1 pound.

Crackers (graham)	48 crackers	. . .	——
Crackers (soda)	80–90 crackers	. . .	——
Cream (thick)—1 pt.	. . .	(4 cups whipped)	——
Dates	2 cups chopped	. . .	——
Eggs (whole)—4–6	1 cup	. . .	——
Fish	. . .	3	——
Flour (white)	4 cups sifted once	. . .	——
Frankfurters	8–10	. . .	——
Gelatin—1 pkg.	2 cups	4	——
Honey—8 oz.	1 cup	. . .	——
Jello—1 pkg.	2 cups	4	——
Lemons—1 med.	3–4 tbsp.	. . .	——
Lettuce	1 head	4 (salads); 8 (garnish)	——
Macaroni—½ lb.	. . .	8	——
Marshmallows	80–90	. . .	——
Nuts: Peanuts	3½ cups	. . .	——
Pecans	3½ cups	. . .	——
Walnuts	4 cups	. . .	——
Oatmeal	6⅔ cups	4	——
Oleomargarine	2 cups	. . .	——
Onions	10–12 onions	. . .	——
Oranges	6	2–3	——
Peaches	3–5	3–5	——
Pears	3–4	3–4	——
Peas in pod	. . .	2–3	——
Potatoes (Irish)	2–4 potatoes	2–4	——
Prunes (dried)	20–40	4–8 (5 per serving)	——
Pudding—3¾ oz.	2 cups	. . .	——
Raisins (seedless)	2–3 cups	. . .	——
Rice	2½ cups	12	——
Salmon—1 can	2½ cups	5	——
Sugar (brown)	2½ cups	. . .	——
Sugar (granulated)	2 cups	. . .	——
Tapioca	2⅔ cups	6–8	——
Tea	6½ cups or 200 bags	200	——
Tomatoes	2–5 tomatoes	4–6	——

(Adapted from National Camp, Matamoras, Pennsylvania. Permission of the late Dr. L. B. Sharp.

APPENDIX L

EQUIPMENT REQUEST

Name of Article	Number	To be used for	To be returned

Requested by_____
Date and Time Wanted_____

By_____

(Adapted from National Camp, Outdoor Education Association, Inc.)

CAMP _____
PROPOSED BUDGET
October 1, _____ through September 30, _____

	19____-____ Proposed Budget (next year)	19____-____ Actual (this year)
INCOME:		

Account No.	Item	Amount
A	Contributions to Camp	
A-1	District I	
A-2	District II	
A-3	District III	
A-4	Campers	
A-5	Others	
B	Camper Fees	
B-1	Regular Camps	
B-2	Other Camps	
C	Store Receipts	
C-1	Store Sales	
C-2	Sales Tax	
D	Income from Farm	
D-1	Rent	
D-2	Other Income	
E	Claims and Refunds	
E-1	Claims-Health Insurance	
E-2	Claims-Other Insurance	
E-3	Federal Milk Reimbursements	
E-4	Other Refunds	
F	Contributions-Transmitted to Other	
G	Sale of Camp Equipment & Supplies	
H	Temporary Loans	
H-1	Interest-free Loans	
H-2	Bank Loans	
H-3	Private Loans with Interest	
I	Other Income	
I-1	Interest-Bonds	
I-2	Interest-Savings	
I-3	Other Income	

TOTAL INCOME:
Cash on Hand, October 1, _____
TOTAL FUNDS PROJECTED:

| | | 19_____-_____ | 19_____-___ |
| **EXPENDITURES:** | | Proposed Budget (next year) | Actual (this year) |

Amount No.	Item	Amount
A	General Control	
A-1	Salary, Manager	
A-2	Salary, Ass't Manager	
A-3	Salary, Accountant	
A-4	Supplies, Manager	
A-5	Printing & Postage	
A-6	Legal Services	
A-7	Other Exp. of General Control	
B	Instructional Program	
B-1	Salaries, Leaders	
B-2	Other Expenses of Leaders	
B-3	Books, Texts, Library	
B-4	Supplies used in Instruction	
B-5	Leadership Conferences	
B-6	Other Exp. of Instruction	
C	Auxiliary Accounts	
C-1	Store Account	
C-1.1	Items Purchased for Resale	
C-1.2	Other Expenses of Store	
C-2	Farm Account	
C-2.1	Fire Insurance	
C-2.2	Taxes	
C-2.3	Other Farm Expenses	
C-3	Funds Transmitted to Other	
D	Operation	
D-1	Custodial	
D-1.1	Salary, Custodian	
D-1.2	Salary, Other Custodial	
D-2	Fuel	
D-3	Light & Power	
D-4	Telephone	
D-5	Custodial Supplies	
D-6	Kitchen Expenses	
D-6.1	Wages of Kitchen Staff	
D-6.2	Food & Supplies	
D-7	Truck & Tractor Costs	
D-7.1	Truck	
D-7.2	Tractor, Chain Saw	
D-8	Medical Expenses	
D-9	Pool	
D-10	Other Exp. of Operation	

		19____-____ Proposed Budget (next year)	19____-___ Actual (this year)
E	Maintenance		
E-1	Upkeep of Grounds		
E-2	Repair of Buildings		
E-3	Heat, Light, Plumbing		
E-4	Furniture		
E-5	Instructional Equipment		
E-6	Other Equipment		
F	Fixed Charges		
F-1	Fire Insurance, Camp		
F-2	Workmen's Compensation		
F-3	Health & Accident Insurance		
F-4	Fidelity Bond Premiums		
F-5	Other Insurance		
G	Debt Service		
G-1	Repayment of Loan Principal		
G-2	Interest on Loans		
H	Capital Outlay		
H-1	Purchase of New Land		
H-2	Improvement of Grounds		
H-3	New Construction		
H-4	Furniture		
H-5	Instructional Apparatus		
H-6	Other Equipment		
J-1	Payroll Account Balance		

TOTAL EXPENSES PROJECTED

Two Major Building Programs in Two Years:
    Cost of Swimming Pool
    Cost of Camp Manager's House

Our Present Indebtedness:
    Valley Trust Company
    Private Loans with Interest
    Interest-free Loans

We Paid This Much

CHURCH CAMP
Comparative Statement of Income & Expenses

INCOME	Year Ending____	Year Ending____
General Income:		
Donations		
Special Dining Hall Receipts		
Miscellaneous Receipts		
Farm Income		
Camp Store and Crafts		
Camp Improvement Fund		
Special Offerings		
Total General Income		
Registrations:		
Church Camps		
Other Denomination Camps		
4-H Camps		
Staff House Weekend Retreats		
Total Registrations		
TOTAL INCOME		
EXPENSES		
Camp Costs:		
Food		
Wages		
Leaders' Expenses		
Director's Expense		
Miscellaneous Expense		
Total Camp Costs		
Administrative Costs:		
Office Supplies		
Electricity		
Telephone		
Fuel		
Insurance		
Annuities		
Auto and Tractor Expenses		
Farm Expenses—seeds, etc.		
Farm Expenses—irrigation system		
Social Security Taxes		
State Sales Taxes		
Repairs on Buildings and Equipment		
Depreciation—Buildings		
Depreciation—Equipment		
Depreciation—Q.M.A.		
Depreciation—Auto and Tractor Equipment		
Depreciation—Farm Irrigation System		
Total Administrative Costs		
TOTAL EXPENSES		
NET PROFIT		

CHURCH CAMP
Statement of Assets & Liabilities

ASSETS

Current Assets:

Cash (checking account)		$ 6,507.97
Petty Cash		75.00
Reserve for Special Projects		582.07
Camp Store and Crafts Inventory		2,945.77
Camp Food Inventory		1,606.70
Unexpired Insurance		1,530.00
Office Supplies Inventory		979.47
Total Current Assets		$ 14,226.98

Fixed Assets:

Land		$ 9,315.00
Buildings as per Appraisal plus Additions	$118,534.01	
Less Reserve for Depreciation	57,328.54	61,205.47
Auditorium as per Appraisal plus Additions	$ 40,000.00	
Less Reserve for Depreciation	27,900.00	12,100.00
Equipment as per Appraisal plus Additions	$ 30,089.96	
Less Reserve for Depreciation	15,840.78	14,249.18
Auto and Tractor Equipment	$ 5,225.00	
Less Reserve for Depreciation	1,637.64	3,587.36
Camp Farm		18,130.00
Farm Irrigation System	$ 3,653.17	
Less Reserve for Depreciation	1,485.48	2,167.69
Total Fixed Assets		$120,754.70

TOTAL ASSETS $134,981.68

LIABILITIES AND NET WORTH

Liabilities:

None

Net Worth:

Church Camp, September 30, ———		$ 125,214.17
Increased—Net Profit, Camp Year———		9,767.51
Church Camp, October 1, ———		$134,981.68

APPENDIX N

SELECTED ABBREVIATED STANDARDS
AMERICAN CAMPING ASSOCIATION

HEALTH

1. Is a physical examination by a licensed physician and a medical history required for all in camp within *three* months *before* camp?
2(V) Is the physical condition of everyone checked immediately before departure for camp or checked upon arrival in camp by physician or registered nurse, licensed to practice in the state in which the examination is conducted?
3(V) Is the report of the physical examination and medical history available at the time of the above check-up?
4. Does the camp require currently valid preventative inoculations as required by public health authorities?
5. Does the camp keep a record of health examinations and statements including any limitations which would affect activities?
6. Is a daily record of first aid and medical treatment of everyone in camp kept by nurse and/or director?
7. Does the camp maintain a definite system of health supervision?
8(V) A. Does the *Family* or *Resident* camp have in residence on its staff a licensed physician and/or registered nurse accredited to practice in the state in which the camp is located?
   B. Does the *Day* camp have a licensed physician on call, a registered nurse or a practical nurse licensed to practice in the state and on the camp site or a person holding a current ARC certificate in advanced first aid on the campsite?
9(V) For *Day, Family* and *Resident* camps. Have arrangements in writing been made for a nearby licensed physician(s) to be on call if one is not in residence?
10(V) Has the camp physician signed standing orders for the nurse?
11(V) Check type of camp: Day_____; Resident_____; Family_____; Travel_____.
   A. In *Day, Family* and *Resident* camps, is there a trained first aid person adequately equipped with first aid supplies prepared by camp nurse or physician to *accompany groups* away from the base camp?
   B. For all camps. Is there a fresh, well supplied first aid kit to serve all transportation units?
   C. Is there one member of the *Travel* camp staff qualified in first aid with a certificate from the Red Cross or its equivalent?
12. Are all staff members given fundamental knowledge of procedure to follow in the event of health emergencies?
13(V) Check type of camp: Family_____; Resident_____. Has the *Family* or *Resident* camp a well equipped infirmary and isolation quarters?
14(V) Is there a first aid area and a quiet resting place set apart from the group at the *Day* camp?
15(V) Is there a planned arrangement for the care of any camper who for any reason must be excluded from the *Travel* camp program for a period of time?
16(V) *Family* and *Resident* camps. Does the camp comply with the Personnel section of the ACA Food Service Sanitation booklet?

17. Does the camp observe nutrition Standards by having its menus planned or approved annually by a qualified nutritionist and/or dietician?
18. Is emergency transportation available at all times?
19(V) Does the camp have ready access to a telephone?
20(V) Does the *Family, Resident* or *Travel* camp have and use hot water facilities for bathing purposes?

SAFETY

1. Is the waterfront program at all times under the direction of an experienced person over 21 years of age who holds a current American Red Cross Water Safety Instructor's certificate or its equivalent from an organization having similar Standards and who is authorized to teach by the local accrediting authority?
2. In addition to the waterfront director, is there on duty a minimum ratio of one person with at least a senior life saving certificate (or its equivalent) per 25 campers in the water?
3. Do practices and equipment for waterfront comply with American Red Cross Standards or those of organizations with equivalent Standards?
4. Is the swimming pool fenced?
5. Do practices and equipment for all watercraft comply with American Red Cross, U.S. Coast Guard Standards or those of other organizations with equivalent Standards?
6. A. Does the riflery program comply with National Rifle Association Standards?
   B. Is the archery program planned and conducted in a manner to provide maximum safety?
   C. Is the riding program planned and conducted in a manner to ensure the safety of all participants?
7. Is special equipment such as boats, outboard motors and firearms brought to camp only with the permission of the director and used in accordance with camp policy and regulations?
8. Are firearms for leaders' emergency use registered and licensed, in compliance with laws?
9. Do two or more counselors accompany groups on out-of-camp trips in accordance with designated ratio?
   Two counselors should be provided for any group of eight campers, plus a ratio of one counselor to each additional eight campers.
10(V) Does the *Family* camp provide two or more program staff members for family camp unit on organized out-of-camp trips, ratio 1 counselor to 20 campers?
11. Before venturing into remote areas, is intent registered with authorities?
12. Are tools and power tools, including safety devices, used and maintained in good repair and used only under qualified supervision?
13. Are gasoline, kerosene, explosives and inflammable materials stored away from buildings used for housing and program and used in a safe manner?
14(V) If water pressure is available, are the lengths of hose adequate for fire fighting in *Day, Family* and *Resident* camps?
15. Are fire extinguishers and other suitable fire fighting equipment placed at strategic and easily accessible points with contents checked prior to and during the camp season?
16(V) Are all fireplaces and chimneys properly built and maintained in good condition in *Day, Family* and *Resident* camps?
17(V) Are arrangements made before the opening of camp with local fire department, fire wardens, forest rangers, etc., for protection in case of fire for *Day, Family* and *Resident* camps?
18. Are all required permits for operation of incinerators and/or for open fires secured in advance?

19(V) Are electric wiring and light fixtures installed in accordance with local building codes or the national Electric Underwriters Association code, and are they maintained in good repair in *Day, Family* and *Resident* camps?
20. Are disaster procedures planned and practiced in the form of drills?

SANITATION

1. Does the camp comply with all local, county and state sanitation laws?
2(V) Does the *Day, Family* or *Resident* camp operate with approved water supply for all purposes?
3. Has the person in charge verified that the water is approved or taken proper steps to render unknown water safe?
4. Is the milk pasteurized or certified by an accredited source?
5. Is storage for milk and perishable foods maintained at a temperature of not over 50°F?
6. Is the storage, preparation, service space, and equipment for food all maintained clean and free from dust and insects?
7. Do dishwashing procedures and care of equipment comply with state, county and local sanitation laws?
8. In the absence of sanitation laws, are effective dish washing procedures in use?
9. Are liquid wastes disposed of through facilities constructed, operated and located as required by supervising state, county, and local health officials?
10. Are toilets adequate in number and in cleanliness?
    Resident and *Family* camps ratio calls for 1 seat for each 10 persons. Male camps with urinals 1 seat for every 15 persons and 1 urinal for every 30.
    Day camps ratio calls for 1 toilet or privy seat for every 20 persons.
    Travel camps ratio is 1 seat for each 10 persons.
11. Are handwashing facilities in proximity to all toilets, privies and urinals?
12(V) Is garbage and rubbish disposal system adequate? (Methods are based on type of camp.)

TRANSPORTATION

1. Is the transportation equipment maintained in safe operating condition?
2. Is there a program of transportation safety education carried on for all camp personnel and adjusted to the transportation practices of the individual camp?
3. Do all persons responsible for operating camp transportation equipment comply with the personal and age qualifications required?
4. Has each camp driver, boat operator and/or pilot a state or federal license indicating his compliance with existing legal regulations and permission to operate such equipment?
5. Are all camp transportation units covered by adequate liability insurance?
6. Does camp carry a hired and a non-owner policy?
7. Do transportation units provide safe seating for each person?
8. Does the camp provide adequate supervision in transportation units?
9. Do chartered transportation units meet ACA transportation Standards?
10. When trailers are used, do they comply with all laws of the various jurisdictions in which travel occurs?
11(V) Does a written plan exist for procedures to be used at highway stops?
12. *Travel* camps. Are relief drivers provided?
13(V) *Travel* camps. Are adequate emergency repair parts and accessories carried by the *Travel* group?

APPENDIX O

STAFF EVALUATION OF CAMP

My Name _____Date_____

Address _____
            (city)   (state and zip)

The camp period I served _____Responsibility_____

1. Evaluate the working relationship with your co-leaders.

2. What do you understand to have been the primary result desired from this camp?

   How well do you feel this was accomplished? ___very well ___somewhat ___little

3. What do you feel made the greatest contribution to the aim of the camp?

   What do you feel made the least contribution to the aim of the camp?

4. What do you feel was your greatest problem as you served? How could you have been helped to answer it?

5. How could the planning committee and director have helped you more?

6. What suggestions do you have
   a) For the purpose of the camp?
   b) For the format and content?
   c) For the selection and preparation of leaders?

7. Please rate the experience of this particular period by checking the appropriate word below. This is an overall evaluation.

Excellent____   Good____   Fair____   Poor____

8. ____I will probably be able to serve again next year. Please contact me after January 1.
   ____I know that I will be unable to serve next year.
   ____I will help to recruit additional staff persons among persons I know, and members of my congregation. Please check with me for names.

APPENDIX P

DIRECTOR'S COUNSELOR EVALUATION SHEET
(Confidential—Directors Only)

Kindly evaluate each counselor in your camp(s) this past summer.

Counselor's Name _____ **Address**_____

No. Weeks served (under your directorship)_____ Age groups_____

Paid counselor? _____yes _____no   Responsibility assignment_____

Rate 0 to 5 (5 = highest rating):
1. Comprehended intent and purpose of the camp_____
2. Able to counsel the camper_____
3. Grew as a person during the period of service_____
4. Degree of stamina—physically_____
5. Degree of maturity—psychologically, mentally, spiritually_____
6. Cooperated with other leaders_____
7. Took initiative when necessary_____
8. Handled discipline problems and commanded respect in so doing_____
9. Showed creativity and imagination_____
10. Responded to positive suggestions from the director_____

Please, in your opinion, rank this person as a counselor, on the basis of performance this summer, using 10 as highest figure, and 0 as lowest:_____

Would you like for this person to serve with you again? _____yes _____no

What notable strengths or notable weaknesses did he have as a leader:_____

_____

_____

Signed,_____
DIRECTOR

Date_____

RESOURCES

I. ADMINISTRATION AND PHILOSOPHY

Decentralized Camping, Lois Goodrich. 1959. 256 pp. $4.75.
  An excellent book on how to carry out decentralized, or small-group, camping.
  Out of print but look for it in church, seminary, and denominational office libraries.

Administration of the Modern Camp, Hedley S. Dimock. 1948. 283 pp. $5.00.
  Staff, health and safety, programming, financial management, food services, maintenance, planning, etc.

The Character Dimension of Camping, Richard Doty. 1960. 192 pp. $4.75.
  Based on ten years of research, a precise description of what happens when a camp sets out to make character outcomes deeper and more certain.

Programs in Outdoor Education, William H. Freeberg and Loren E. Taylor. Burgess Publishing Company, 1963. 457 pp. $6.00.
  Offers principles for guidance and types of program, and suggests ways of enriching subject matter through outdoor education.

The Successful Camp, Lewis C. Reimann. 1958. 233 pp. $4.75.
  A discussion of practically every aspect of camp administration, from the site to staff and camper morale.

A Handbook on Quantity Food Management, E. Evelyn Smith. Burgess Publishing Company, 1955. $4.00.
  Written primarily for classes in institutional management; useful to camp dietitians for food service management; work organization, use and care of equipment, safety.

Swimming Pool Management—A Manual on Sanitation, Filtration, and Disinfection, Charles C. Stott. American Institute of Park Executives, 1965.
  Management Aids (Bulletin No. 50).

Job Descriptions of Positions in a Camp, David B. Dabrow. Mimeo. 100 pp. $3.50.
  (Order from American Camping Association, Martinsville, Indiana 46151.)

The Camp Nurse, Health and Safety Committee, American Camping Association. 1956. 25 pp. 50¢.
  A guide to camp nursing and the total health program. Highly recommended for every camp nurse.

Recipes for Quantity Service, U. S. Department of Agriculture. Government Printing Office, 1961.
  Prepared by Human Nutrition Division, Agricultural Research Service. Laboratory tested recipes in quantities of 25, 50, and 100 portions.

Wilderness Road, Campbell Loughmiller. Hogg Foundation for Mental Health, Austin, Texas, 1956. 139 pp. $2.50 (*out of print*).
  The story of a man and his camp for rehabilitating boys. Excellent for all camp leaders to read and ponder.

Growing Inside, Outside, Bud Harper. The United Church of Canada, Board of Christian Education, 1969.
  A book of guidelines for church camping produced by the United Church of Canada.

II. SITE SELECTION AND DEVELOPMENT

Site Selection and Development: Camps, Conferences, Retreats. Bone, Britten, Brown, Davis, and Schlingman. 1965. 174 pp. $12.50.
 Comprehensive and authoritative guide on master planning, factors in site selection, land use and management, facilities, administration and finances.
Developing Camp Sites and Facilities. John A. Ledlie, editor. 1960. 63 pp. $3.50.
 An illustrated manual of check lists and layouts for over-all planning and development of camp ground and facilities: living quarters, kitchen, waterfront, and health and sanitation.
Camp Site Development. Julian H. Salomon. Girl Scouts of the U.S.A., 1959. Catalog 19–527. $3.00.
 Covers all aspects from choice of site to design of buildings.
Campsites and Facilities. Boy Scouts of America, 1950. 194 pp. $7.50.
 Discussion of the many factors involved in the selection and development of camp facilities.

III. COUNSELING

Training Camp Counselors in Human Relations. Jerry Beker. 1962. 186 pp. $3.75.
 An approach to tension-building situations in camp. Forty-two case histories which can be used to great advantage in training sessions.
A Camp Director Trains His Own Staff, Catherine T. Hammett. American Camping Association, 1947. 32 pp. 50¢.
 Suggestions for pre- and in-camp training. Excellent for camp directors.
The Miracle of Dialogue. Reuel L. Howe. 1963. 154 pp. $1.65 (paper).
 Process of communication basic to the Christian community.
Learning Together in the Christian Fellowship. Sara Little. 1956. 104 pp. $1.25 (paper).
 Methods of study, evaluation, motivation, and learning. Participation while learning together.
Learning to Work in Groups: A Program Guide for Educational Leaders. Matthew B. Miles. Teacher's College Press, New York, N.Y., 1959. $2.25 (paper).
 Skills for working effectively in small groups, training procedures. Beamed at public education but broadly applicable.
Camp Counseling. A. Viola Mitchell and Ida B. Crawford. W. B. Saunders Co., 3rd edition, 1961. 412 pp. $6.25.
 The camp counselor's job. Objectives; self-rating scale; understanding the camper; camp activities.
So You Want to Be a Camp Counselor. Elmer F. Ott. 1946. 112 pp. $1.25 (paper).
 Camp counselor qualifications and responsibilities.

IV. CONSERVATION AND ECOLOGY

The Web of Life. John H. Storer. New American Library, 1956. 128 pp. 75¢.
 A first book of ecology, presenting in readable form the story of the interrelationship of all living things. Excellent.
The First Book of Conservation. Frances C. Smith. Franklin Watts, Inc., 1954. 70 pp. $2.65.
 The story of the interrelationship of all of life, of what man has and has not done to renew natural resources, and of what he may do. Well illustrated. Large print for easy reading.
Field Trips: Ecology for Youth Leaders. Janet Nickelsburg. Burgess Publishing Company, 1966. 120 pp. $2.75.

An introduction to areas and methods in ecological studies. Should be studied by leaders before camp.

Reading the Landscape. May Theilgaard Watts. 1964. 230 pp. $5.95.
Climate, animals, and man have their effects on the growing things of an area. Mrs. Watts demonstrates how to recreate the history of many regions by their revealing plant life. Excellent.

The Quiet Crisis. Stewart L. Udall. Avon, 1964. 224 pp. 95¢ (paper).
An attempt to outline the land-and-people story of America, and dedicated to the proposition that men must grasp completely the relationship between human stewardship and the fullness of the American earth.

Silent Spring. Rachel Carson. Fawcett, 1964. 368 pp. 75¢.
A courageous treatment of man's attempt to beat nature through indiscriminate use of lethal chemicals, and the resulting death of innocent life.

V. CAMPING

The Camp Program Book. Catherine T. Hammett and Virginia Musselman. 1951. 380 pp. $5.95.
Camp program in relation to the camper; how camp activities develop out of a natural situation; group leadership utilized for indigenous program; extensive help in specific fields.

Fundamentals of Day Camping. Grace Mitchell. 1961. 256 pp. $4.50.
A very concise, well-organized, and most helpful guide dealing with the site, administration, food, staff, and program.

The Day Camp Program Book. Virginia W. Musselman. 1963. 384 pp. $7.95.
An omnibus resource book for ages 5–12 years.

So You Want to Start a Day Camp. American Camping Association, Inc., 1964. $1.25.

Going Light, with Backpack or Burro. David R. Brower, editor. Sierra Club, San Francisco, 1951 (sixth printing, 1960). 152 pp. $2.50.
Experienced hikers and packers have written an excellent book adaptable for church trail hikes.

Canoe Camping: A Guide to Wilderness Travel. Carle W. Handel. 1956. 192 pp. $4.00.
A veteran adventurer describes in detail the correct way to plan and carry out a canoe camping trip.

Canoeing. American Red Cross. 1956. 445 pp. $1.25.
An outstanding manual on the subject, well illustrated.

Guide to Campsites. C. S. Hammond and Co., Maplewood, N.J.

Your Family Goes Camping. Doris T. Pattterson. 1959.

Family Activities with Other Families. Helen F. Southard. National Board, YWCA, New York.

Sunset Family Camping. Editorial staffs of Sunset Books and Sunset Magazine. Revised, 1962. 128 pp. $1.95.
Three categories: Planning a grand adventure; assembling camp equipment; life in camp. Useful for trip camping for any age group.

Church Family Camps and Conferences. Elizabeth and W. H. Genné. 1962. Paper. $1.40.
A thorough administrative and program manual.

The Handbook of Wilderness Travel. George and Iris Wells. 1956. $4.00. (*out of print*)
A comprehensive survey of wilderness areas in the United States, with information on camping, packing, canoe and float travel, jeep, and swamp buggy.

Book of Outdoor Winter Activities. Harry D. Edgren and Gunnar A. Peterson. 1962. $4.50.

How-to-do-it suggestions for winter experiences in the out-of-doors; hobbies and trail hiking.

Cooking Out-of-Doors. Girl Scouts of the U.S.A. 1960. Catalog 19–533. $2.50.
A cook book that covers many details of outdoor requirements for cooking, with recipes based on twelve persons. Very good.

VI. NATURE CRAFTS AND STUDY

Stepping Stones to Nature. R. O. Bale. Burgess Publishing Company, 1960. 120 pp. $3.00.
Directions for dozens of craft activities. Most require little or no equipment. All use nature materials.

Creative Crafts for Campers. Catherine T. Hammett and Carol M. Horrocks. 1957. $7.95.
One hundred seventy-five projects making use of materials found on most camp-sites.

Your Own Book of Campcraft. Catherine T. Hammett. Pocket Books, Inc., 1950. 197 pp. 50¢.
For campers and counselors. Guidance on outdoor equipment, campcraft skills, fire-making, outdoor foods, lashing, tool craft, compassing, exploration.

Creative Nature Crafts. Robert O. Bale. Burgess Publishing Company, 1959. 120 pp. $3.00.
Many craft projects using native materials are clearly defined and illustrated.

Nature Crafts. Ellsworth Jaeger. 1949. 128 pp. $3.95.
Many crafts of native materials are described which could be survival aids and other fun articles. Excellently illustrated.

Wildwood Wisdom. Ellsworth Jaeger. 1945. $5.95. Fully illustrated guides, useful and practical for perfecting camp and woodcraft skills.

Be Expert with Map and Compass. Bjorn Kjellstrom. Silva, Inc., 1961. 136 pp. $2.60.
Basic knowledge of map and compass reading. Usable for older campers as well as leaders. Attractive in style. Illustrated.

Golden Nature Guides. Golden Press. $1.00 each (paper)
Attractive, pocket-size books. Well illustrated in color and with accurate information.

Birds	Mammals	Stars
Fishes	Pond Life	Trees
Flowers	Reptiles and Amphibians	Weather
Fossils	Rocks and Minerals	
Insects	Seashores	

Field Guide Series, edited by Roger Tory Peterson. $4.95 each (paper).
One of the more detailed studies in each field, yet easily understood.

Birds	Mammals	Reptiles and Amphibians
Western Birds	Rocks and Minerals	Trees and Shrubs
Shells	Animal Tracks	Rocky Mountain
Butterflies	Ferns	Wildflowers

How to Know the Birds. R. T. Peterson. New American Library, 1957. 168 pp. 60¢.
Simple aid to bird recognition. Seventy-two full color illustrations, over 400 drawings.

How to Know the Ferns. Frances Theoroda Parsons. Dover Publications, 1899. 2nd edition. $1.50.
Guide to names, haunts, and habits of our common ferns.

Flower Finder. May T. Watts. Nature Study Guild, Naperville, Ill., 1955. 64 pp. 50¢. (*out of print*)
> Sixty-four page key to more than 200 kinds of wild flowers (Eastern United States). Good for field identification.

How to Know the Wild Flowers. Mrs. William Starr Dana. Dover Publications, 1963. $2.00.
> More than 1,000 wild flowers of the Eastern and Central United States and Canada.

Boy's Book of Snakes. P. A. Morris. 1948. 185 pp. $4.50.
> Leads to understanding of non-poisonous snakes and the few poisonous snakes in this country. Full explanation of coloring and habits.

Stargazing. Janet Nickelsburg. Burgess Publishing Company, 1964. 99 pp. $3.25. (*Out of print.*)
> Especially for the amateur instructor: how to introduce young people to the study of heavenly bodies. Untechnical; legends from many sources.

Evening Sky Star Maps. C. Milton Jaycox, Duvall Rd., Route 2, Woodbine, Maryland 21797. 1934. $1.25.
> Set of four charts, one for each season.

Master Tree Finder, May T. Watts. Nature Study Guild, Naperville, Ill., 1939. (*Out of print.*)
> Key for identification of trees by their leaves. Pocket-size edition. Useful in the East.

A Pocket Guide to Trees, Rutherford Platt. Washington Square, 1960. 75¢ (paper).
> How to identify and enjoy trees.

How to Know the Trees, H. E. Jaques. William C. Brown Company, 1946. 166 pp. $2.50 (paper).
> A detailed and clear tree key study for identifying trees.

Junior Book of Camping and Wood Craft, Bernard S. Mason. 1943. 120 pp. $4.50.
> By word and picture the crafts are made so clear that one cannot miss them.

VII. WORSHIP

Worship Ways for Camp, Clarice Bowman. 1955. 182 pp. $4.50. (*Out of print.*)
> More than 200 worship aids to help make spiritual values real with young people.

Altars Under the Sky, Dorothy Wells Pease. 1957. 159 pp. $2.50.
> Suggested services of worship; excellent as resource materials.

Inspiration Under the Sky, Dorothy Wells Pease. 1963. 140 pp. $2.00.
> Arranged around seven themes on nature, this anthology expresses an undeniable awareness of the magnificent creativeness and glorious presence of God.

Meditations for Youth, Walter L. Cook. 1958. 112 pp. $1.75.
> A book of meditations that contains refreshment, challenge, and renewal for the spirit.

Think About These Things, Jane Merchant. 1956. 96 pp. $2.00.
> Eighty-six meditations, using her own poems and prayers with Scriptual selections, reveal the writer's sense of interrelationship with God's natural creation, as well as a depth of human understanding. Excellent resource material for camp leaders.

VIII. GAMES AND STORY TELLING

Omnibus of Fun, Helen and Larry Eisenberg. 1956. 625 pp. $7.95.
> An antidote for the dull moments; filled with thousands of "instant-activities."

American Folk Tales and Songs, Compiled by Richard Chase. New American Library, 1956. 240 pp. 75¢.
> Tales, ballads, hymns, games, folk customs.

Grandfather Tales, Richard Chase. 1948. 240 pp. $5.00.
Folk tales from the mountains of western North Carolina.
The Jack Tales, Richard Chase. 1943. 202 pp. $3.75.
Tales collected from the mountains of western North Carolina and Wise County, Va. (grades 4–7).

IX. FILMSTRIPS

Camping with Junior Highs, 35mm, 88-frame color filmstrip with script. $5.00.
Order from denominational bookstore.
Day Camping for Your Church, 35mm, 47-frame color filmstrip with script. $7.50.
Order from Cokesbury.

X. CHURCH CAMPING

1. Cooperatively Planned Materials

Living and Learning in God's World, LaDonna Bogardus. 1961. 224 pp. $2.00.
Comprehensive guidance for day camps and resident camps for 4th–6th graders. Program resources valuable for family camping. (Three books for campers accompany this book: *We Adventure in God's World,* Goddard; *We Discover in God's World,* Venable; *We Explore in God's World,* Davis; 50¢ each. They include suggestions for the small camp, menus and recipes, directions for things to make, games, and materials for worship.)
Camping Together as Christians, John and Ruth Ensign. 1958. 148 pp. $1.50.
Brings together in a book for leaders of 7th–9th graders three major program emphases in church camping: Christian community, Christian stewardship, and Christian growth. (Three books for campers accompany this: *My Camp Book: Christian Community,* Morton; *My Camp Book: Christian Stewardship,* Ensigns; *Let's Go Camping,* Laughmillers; 40¢ each.)

The "Let's Series," published by the National Council of Churches of Christ.
These five booklets are designed to help leaders with six-to-twelve-year-olds in their Christian education outdoors. They may be used as supplemental material for junior camps.
Let's Go Exploring. Leo Rippy, Jr., 1959. 32 pp. 60¢.
Let's Play. LaDonna Bogardus, 1958. 48 pp. 70¢.
Let the Bible Speak Outdoors, Mary Elizabeth Mason, 1962. 47 pp. 70¢.
Let's Find Outdoor Opportunities for Worship. Barbara P. Poppe, 1960. 43 pp. 60¢.
Let's Teach Through Group Relations. Dorothy W. Caton, 1959. 64 pp. $1.00.

2. American Baptist Church

(Order from: Board of Christian Education and Publication, American Baptist Convention, Valley Forge, Pennsylvania 19481)

God Speaks to Me! Ernst E. Klein. Judson Press, $1.75.
Counselor's guide for juniors. "Nature is the great book in which God is constantly writing of his power, glory, and goodness." Twenty-nine discoveries are suggested to spark imagination and activities. (Camper book of same title and author.)

3. The Christian Church (Disciples of Christ)

(Order from: Christian Board of Publication, Box 179, St. Louis, Missouri 63166)

The Junior High Camp, Ralph Stone.
A manual to help adults understand the nature and philosophy of church camps and their role in them.
Inheritor of the World. Dennis Savage.
Leader's guide on the theme, living responsibly in the world God has made. (Camper book by the same title.)
Behold! God. Harry Baker Adams and Manette Adams.
Leader's guide on the theme, discovering God's self-disclosure and responding to God. (Camper book by same title.)
Sincerely Yours, Donald F. Clingan.
Leader's guide on the theme, living with integrity in our dealings with one another. (Camper book by same title.)
The Senior High Conference, Cy Rowell.
The basic guide to leaders in senior high conferences.
The Great Belonging, D. Campbell Wyckoff.
Leader's guide on the theme, living as sons of God in the church. (Conferee's book by same title.)
In His Image, Mary Ellen Prime.
Leader's guide on the theme, fulfillment of the self as a son of God. (Conferee's book by same title.)
A Cup of Water, Charles H. Bayer, Jr.
Leader's guide on the theme, living as sons of God in society. (Conferee's book by same title.)
No Greater Love, Paul A. Crow, Jr.
Leader's guide on the theme, discovering the message and meaning of the Christian command. (Conferee's book by same title.)

4. The Lutheran Church in America

(Order from: Board of Parish Education, Lutheran Church in America, 2900 Queen Lane, Philadelphia, Pennsylvania 19129)

Church Camp Administration, Paul M. Cornell.
Church Camp Program Guide—Grades 4–6, Elizabeth M. Purdham.
Leader's guide for understanding and developing the camp program with suggestions for activities.
It Takes Courage, Sherley G. Ruby.
Leader's guide on the theme, discovering the nature of Christian courage and Christian resources. (Camper book by the same title.)
The Trouble Is . . ., Eleanor M. Mathews.
Leader's guide on the theme, learning how to cope with problem spots. (Camper book by the same title.)
Echoes of His Way, Helen Mason.
Leader's guide on the theme, relating one's understanding of God to knowledge and experience of creation. (Camper book by the same title.)
Church Camp Program Guide—Grades 7–9, Russell E. Fink
To help leaders create programs that will be effective instruments of Christian education.
Finding My Way, Inez Seagle.
Leader's guide on the theme, discovering how a camper's relationship with God

should influence relationships with parents and peers. (Camper book by the same title.)

Listening to God, Walter L. Brandau.
Leader's guide on the theme, seeing and hearing how God speaks and how each should respond to him. (Camper book by the same title.)

Living in Christ, Lucille E. Hein and Walter A. Kortrey.
Leader's guide on the theme, viewing myself as created and redeemed by God and called to a life of service. (Camper book by the same title.)

Church Camp Program Guide—Grades 10–12, Paul E. Carl.
Helps for the camp director as he plans and directs a church camp for senior highs.

We Believe, Elizabeth Kidd.
A survey of the basic teachings of the Christian church. (Camper book by the same title.)

We Witness, Russell E. Fink.
Teacher's guide for Christian witnessing as a way of life. (Camper book by the same title.)

We Serve, Frank P. Grobelny.
Teacher's guide on the theme, what does God want me to do with the life he gave me? (Camper book by the same title.)

Church Camp Counselor's Manual—Grades 4–6, Elizabeth V. Shealy.
Directed to the cabin counselor with suggestions in crafts, recreation, nature lore, etc.

Church Camp Counselor's Manual—Grades 7–9, David Belgum.
Directed to the cabin counselor, taking into consideration varieties of camp settings and scheduling.

Church Camp Counselor's Manual—Grades 10–12, Jerry L. Schmalenberger.
Directed to the entire staff of a 10–12th grades camp or conference.

5. The United Methodist Church

(Order from: General Board of Education, The United Methodist Church, Box 871, Nashville, Tennessee 37202)

"Training Leaders in Camping"—a packet of materials issued annually.
When Your Family Goes Camping, Ralph Bugg.
A basic manual for individual families who go camping on their own.

6. The Presbyterian Church in the United States

(Order from: The Board of Christian Education, Presbyterian Church U.S., Box 1176, Richmond, Virginia 23209)

The Earth Is the Lord's, Mary Jean McFadyen
Leader's guide for grades 5–6 in small group camping with two study themes, God at work in his world, and God's people enjoying his world.

Camping in Covenant Community, Geneva Giese.
The leader's guide for small group camping with grades 7–8, with two themes, in covenant community, and how God reveals himself.

This Company of New Men: A Study of the Thessalonian Church, B. Frank Hall.
The leader's guide designed for small group study, with senior high youth in camp or conference setting.

What's Right, C. Ellis Nelson.
Leader's guide for a study of the Ten Commandments, with senior high youth in camp or conference setting.

Confronted by Christ, Cecil Culverhouse.
Leader's guide for study of selected passages from the Gospel of John, with senior high youth in a camp or conference setting.
Recreation in the Out-of-Doors.
Suggestions for recreation suitable for camps, conferences, and the local church groups.

7. The United Church of Christ

(Order from: Camps and Conferences, United Church Board for Homeland Ministries, 1505 Race Street, Philadelphia, Pennsylvania 19102)

Junior High Camp-Conference Manual on Christian Stewardship.
Junior High Camp-Conference Manual on Christian Growth.
The Recreation Job in Camp and Conference, Edward L. Schlingman. 77 pp. 50¢.
For the Quizzical—Quizzes and Contests Are Fun, Paul C. Scheirer, compiler and editor. 30 pp.
A resource book on recreation.
Let's Relay It—A Collection of Relays, Edward L. Schlingman, compiler. 19 pp.
Let's Play Outdoors—A Manual of Outdoor Activities and Games, Edward L. Schlingman. 17 pp.

8. The United Presbyterian Church in the United States of America

(Order from: The Geneva Press, United Presbyterian Church U.S.A., Witherspoon Building, Philadelphia, Pennsylvania 19107)

Cues for Church Camping.
An excellent book for counselors of juniors and junior highs in small group camping.
Seeking Meaning with Junior Highs in Camp, C. F. Messinger and G. F. Ulrich.
A camp program book for leaders with junior highs having three themes: discovering meaning in worship, in the natural environment, and in themselves.

ACKNOWLEDGMENTS

1. Lois Goodrich, *Decentralized Camping: A Handbook* (New York: Association Press, 1959), p. 21.

2. *Standards Report for the Accreditation of Organized Camps* (Martinsville, Ind.: American Camping Association, 1966), p. vii.

3. Virginia W. Musselman, *The Day Camp Program Book* (New York: Association Press, 1963), p. 18.

4. *Standards Report for the Accreditation of Organized Camps, op. cit.*

5. Goodrich, *op. cit.*, p. vii.

6. Hedley S. Dimock, editor, *Administration of the Modern Camp* (New York: Association Press, 1948), pp. 93–94.

7. Maurice D. Bone, and others, *Site Selection and Development Camps-Conferences-Retreats* (Philadelphia: United Church Press, 1965), p. 14.

37790